P9-DBI-536

Beaded Chain Mail Jewelry

Beaded Chain Mail Jewelry
Timeless Techniques with a Twist

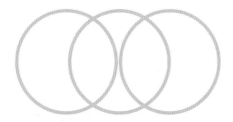

Dylon Whyte

LARK BOOKS
A Division of Sterling Publishing Co., Inc.
New York / London

739.27
WHY

SENIOR EDITOR
Terry Taylor

EDITOR
Larry Shea

ASSISTANT EDITOR
Mark Bloom

ART DIRECTOR
Stacey Budge

PHOTOGRAPHER
Stewart O'Shields

COVER DESIGNER
Chris Bryant

mw

Library of Congress Cataloging-in-Publication Data

Whyte, David Dylon, 1974-
  Beaded chain mail jewelry : timeless techniques with a twist / David Dylon
Whyte. – 1st ed.
       p. cm.
  Includes index.
  ISBN 978-1-60059-220-1 (HC-PLC with jacket : alk. paper)
  1. Jewelry making. 2. Metal-work. 3. Chains (Jewelry) 4. Beadwork. I.
Title.
  TT212.W49 2009
  739.27–dc22
                                          2008017831

10 9 8 7 6 5 4 3 2 1

First Edition

Published by Lark Books, A Division of
Sterling Publishing Co., Inc.
387 Park Avenue South, New York, NY 10016

Text and illustrations © 2008, David Dylon Whyte
Photography © 2008, Lark Books unless otherwise specified

Distributed in Canada by Sterling Publishing,
c/o Canadian Manda Group, 165 Dufferin Street
Toronto, Ontario, Canada M6K 3H6

Distributed in the United Kingdom by GMC Distribution Services,
Castle Place, 166 High Street, Lewes, East Sussex, England BN7 1XU

Distributed in Australia by Capricorn Link (Australia) Pty Ltd.,
P.O. Box 704, Windsor, NSW 2756 Australia

The written instructions, photographs, designs, patterns, and projects in this volume are
intended for the personal use of the reader and may be reproduced for that purpose
only. Any other use, especially commercial use, is forbidden under law without written
permission of the copyright holder.

Every effort has been made to ensure that all the information in this book is accurate.
However, due to differing conditions, tools, and individual skills, the publisher cannot be
responsible for any injuries, losses, and other damages that may result from the use of
the information in this book.

If you have questions or comments about this book, please contact:
Lark Books
67 Broadway
Asheville, NC 28801
828-253-0467

Manufactured in China

All rights reserved

ISBN 13: 978-1-60059-220-1

For information about custom editions, special sales, premium and corporate purchas-
es, please contact Sterling Special Sales Department at 800-805-5489 or specialsales@
sterlingpub.com.

Contents

Introduction

Hello, my name is Dylon Whyte, and I am a chain mail addict.

After more than 20 years of creating, researching, and teaching about chain mail, I have literally seen more than two million jump rings pass between the jaws of my pliers. I've made just about every type of chain mail project you can imagine, from recreations of medieval clothing that weigh many pounds and contain 100,000 jump rings, to the most delicate earrings containing just a few.

As my knowledge of chain mail and its patterns—both those I've discovered from history and those I've invented on my own—has grown, I've been drawn more and more to designing smaller, more detailed pieces. In particular, I now love creating what I'll share with you in this book: elegant jewelry that combines intricate chain mail with glorious beads.

Whether you're a chain mail enthusiast, a beader discovering jump rings for the first time, or just someone looking for a new horizon in jewelry making, you'll find the techniques here easy to learn and the projects fun to make. The Basics section begins with detailed information about the types and materials of jump rings and beads you'll use, followed by information on the essential tools you'll need—two pairs of pliers—and a few other helpful tools and materials.

I'll next show you how to create eight basic chain weaves you'll be using throughout the book. Some are adaptations of old favorites, such as European 1 in 4 and Byzantine, while others include my original patterns Rings of Saturn and Persian Star. Every weave is accompanied by step-by-step instructions and numerous detailed illustrations to get you up to speed for creating any of the 26 projects that follow.

These projects merge ancient chain patterns going back thousands of years with contemporary styles. Necklaces such as Drops of Jupiter (page 65) and Nautilus (page 136) are as elegant and original as anything you would find in an upscale jewelry store. The adaptable Arrowhead Wrap (page 76) is both traditional and punk. Men are often left behind when it comes to jewelry style, and I've tried to correct that oversight with the classy Bronze Age Bolo Tie (page 116) and the boot, key, and wallet chains that join up in the Chain Gang project (page 91).

Other projects—like the set of bails in the Connection Quartet (page 48) and the multiple Zipper Charms (page 120)—show how you can ring a set of variations on a theme through changing the weave, the materials, or the beads you use. Don't be limited, though, by the variations I've suggested. Throughout the book, look for places where you can make substitutions and adaptations to let your imagination shine. In the mood for something chic? Replacing jump rings with sterling silver ones or beads with pearlescent pebbles might do the trick. Is something more tribal to your taste? In that case, use copper jump rings and wooden or clay beads to create a brand-new funky masterpiece.

The great thing about the time-tested techniques you'll find in this book is this: It doesn't matter how familiar you are with jewelry making, or even if you've never picked up a pair of pliers before in your life. Just read the directions carefully, practice the basic techniques, and you will be making your own chain mail projects in no time at all. Each and every piece here was made with love and a passion for creativity. I hope you enjoy discovering the inner secrets of these jewelry pieces as much as I enjoyed bringing them to life.

The Basics

Chains have been woven into patterns and used both practically and decoratively for thousands of years. It's thought that the Celts were the first to wear expanded chain weaves known as *mail* for armor.

Mail is often called *chain mail, chainmaille,* or *maille*; this last term pays homage to the early Old French roots of the word. All these terms are basically redundant, however, as the direct translation of "maille" is "chain"—so using *chain mail* or *chainmaille* is like saying "chain chain" or "mail mail." However, the term "chain mail" is often preferred to avoid confusion with the mail that gets delivered to your house.

All of the jewelry projects in this book contain some form of chain. For the sake of simplicity, I'll refer to all chain and chain weave patterns simply as chains.

You need three things to construct a chain in its most basic form: two pairs of pliers and a supply of jump rings. The following sections discuss pliers and jump rings in depth, as well as a smattering of other tools that can make your chain-creating experience easier. Since the focus of this book is on beaded chains, I'll also discuss the kinds of beads you can use in chain construction.

JUMP RINGS

Jump rings are formed by coiling wire around a mandrel and then cutting the coil along one side to create metal rings. The direction you wrap the coil determines the left or right offset of the jump ring. Jump rings with a right offset are said to be more appropriate for right-handed chain makers. I've found, though, that offset preference is usually determined by whichever offset a chain maker first encounters (figure 1).

Counterclockwise
(left handed)

Clockwise
(right handed)

FIGURE 1

The two factors that determine the size of a jump ring are the diameter of the mandrel on which the wire was wound, called the *inner diameter* (ID); and the thickness of the wire, known as its *gauge* (figure 2). Both of these factors can be somewhat confusing because some materials spring back slightly when they're cut. The actual ID, therefore, is often slightly larger than the mandrel, meaning that different materials will vary in ID size. Wire gauges can also vary in thickness due to manufacturing differences.

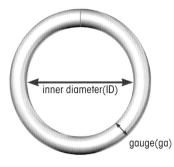

inner diameter(ID)

gauge(ga)

FIGURE 2

I constructed all of the projects in this book from jump rings available from two commercial sources. In each project, I'll give you the individual jump ring sizes required. In the back of the book, I tell you which source provided the rings for each project. If you want to make your own jump rings or purchase pre-made jump rings from other sources, check the gauge chart on page 143. You can also refer to the specific manufacturer's websites for information on their specific sizing methods.

The highest quality jump rings are cut with a *low kerf* saw. The kerf is the width of the groove made by a cutting tool. With jump rings, this is the space between the offset ends of the ring. If this space is too great, the rings can look distorted when closed. Jump rings cut by mechanical means have very rough edges and are generally unsuitable for jewelry-making purposes.

Saw-cut rings, depending on the material and the saw used, can sometimes have burrs. Burrs are usually best removed by tumbling the rings (page 21) either before or after the construction of jewelry pieces. All jewelry-quality jump rings come pre-tumbled.

Jump Ring Materials

Jump rings are made from many different materials. Those most suitable for chain mail jewelry are listed below, but in general, try to avoid less expensive materials. Cheap rings often have nickel plating, which deteriorates rapidly. Mild steel rusts when it touches skin. Galvanized steel, while inexpensive, tarnishes when exposed to skin and forms a scummy patina that can't be cleaned. Also, avoid using "blackened steel" products, as they have a highly unstable finish.

STERLING SILVER

Often called "925 Silver," this material contains 92.5 percent pure silver and, in the highest quality samples, 7.5 percent pure copper. The sterling silver wire used for jump rings comes in several types: *dead soft, half hard,* and *spring hard,* all of which refer to how much the material has been "work hardened." In thicker gauges, half hard sterling is perfectly acceptable, but for smaller gauges, spring hard sterling best retains its strength. Regardless of which you choose, use smooth jaw or padded jaw pliers to avoid leaving tool marks on the rings.

Recently, tarnish-free or tarnish-resistant sterling silver has become available. These amalgams replace the 7.5 percent copper with combinations of other rare metals such as germanium. These materials are suitable for chain jewelry; however, they can be hard to obtain and are often more expensive than regular sterling silver.

Sterling silver and copper jump rings

COPPER

Pure copper is the heaviest material used for jump rings. It is an excellent alternative to more expensive materials. Copper comes in several hardness types, but it is always slightly softer than silver, so be careful to avoid tool marks.

Pure copper tarnishes quickly, dulls over time, and takes on a robust and possibly desirable chocolate brown patina when worn regularly. *Enamelled copper* jump rings are available in a wide range of vivid colors. These rings are almost always manufactured from dead soft copper wire, so handle them carefully both during and after construction. See Keeping It Clean below for ways to protect enamelled surfaces from damage.

KEEPING IT CLEAN

Metals such as sterling silver, copper, bronze, and brass tarnish when exposed to the atmosphere. You can delay tarnishing by storing these metals with commercial anti-tarnish strips or a small chunk of chalk. To clean lightly tarnished metals, soak the pieces for five to ten minutes in pure lemon juice, rinse them in clean water, and pat them dry.

To remove heavier tarnish, lightly scrub the piece with toothpaste and a toothbrush, then rinse it clean. For heavy tarnish, you can usually find material-specific chemical and abrasive tarnish removers.

Be careful not to damage your jump rings by excessive tugging. Also, since you can damage bead and stone materials with certain chemicals, test all cleaning materials before applying them to a finished or valuable piece!

GOLD FILLED

This material offers a relatively inexpensive alternative to real gold. Gold filled wire has a core of sterling silver bonded to a layer of 14-karat gold. To qualify as gold filled, the 14-karat gold must account for 5 percent of the total thickness or volume. These rings are more durable than standard gold-plated rings, making them better suited for chain jewelry.

Gold filled jump rings are as hard as sterling silver. Use smooth jaw pliers and treat the metal gently. While much less expensive than pure gold, gold filled is still more expensive than most chain jewelry material.

Gold-filled and brass jump rings

BRASS

An amalgam of copper and zinc, brass can contain anywhere between 60 to 85 percent copper and 15 to 40 percent zinc. High-zinc brass, often called *yellow brass*, tends to look very yellow and is only slightly harder than pure copper. High-copper brass—called *jewelry brass, red brass*, or even *Merlin's Gold*—has a reddish gold tone and is much harder than copper and yellow brass. Jewelry brass is the most suitable for chain jewelry, although it does tend to tarnish quickly. Clean it often, as you would silver and copper.

BRIGHT ALUMINUM

This material, derived from common bauxite, is both shiny and durable. Less than half the weight of steel, it makes very light chain jewelry. Bright aluminum offers a pure silver tone. (Even sterling silver can't compare.) Since bright aluminum can tarnish over time, give it a good scrub with regular dish soap. It is an excellent material with which to learn chain construction, as it is inexpensive and easy to work with.

Expect bright aluminum jump rings to be harder and springier than precious metal jump rings. While slightly more resistant to tool marks, these rings can also be harder to close smoothly.

Aluminum is often colored by placing the metal in a dye bath after being *anodized*, an electrolytic process that helps the surface better absorb the dye. Anodizing can provide a rainbow of colors; however, the anodized surface is fragile—take care not to scratch it. The best anodized jump rings have colored ends. The surface coloring of cheaper anodized jump rings is much less stable.

Bright aluminum jump rings

BRONZE

This material is an amalgam of 98 percent copper and 2 percent tin. Bronze is much harder than copper, jewelry brass, and even bright aluminum. With a spring characteristic similar to stainless steel, bronze is an excellent material when you want copper but need a stronger and lighter chain.

Bronze tarnishes more slowly than pure copper but in a nearly identical manner. Clean it using the same methods as silver and pure copper.

STAINLESS STEEL

This metal—containing various amounts of iron, carbon, nickel, and other components—is the undisputed king of inexpensive chain-making materials. Stainless steel is hard and springy; it often requires a lot of strength and robust pliers to work.

Because of its variable composition, stainless has a slight color variance—anywhere from a dull gray to a bright bluish tone to a slight yellow undertone. Stainless steel rarely exhibits any sort of tarnish. Clean it with dish soap, or simply pop it in the dishwasher.

So-called *surgical stainless steel* is often sold as hypoallergenic, as it contains far less nickel than regular stainless steel. Individuals with nickel allergies should still be careful, though, as only Europe has actual nickel content standards for products labelled hypoallergenic.

Bronze and stainless steel jump rings, with neoprene rubber rings

NEOPRENE

While not available as jump rings, these durable synthetic rubber rings can be purchased in the form of multicolored O-rings that nicely match several sizes of jump rings. Neoprene rings are useful for chain weaves when you want to have a little extra stretch. A synthetic rubber, neoprene rings are U.V. safe, waterproof, and hypoallergenic.

NIOBIUM

You can find this rare metal in only a few small sizes of anodized jump rings. It is considered completely hypoallergenic. Anodized niobium tends to be less colorful than anodized aluminum due to its dark gray base color. It is similar in hardness to stainless steel, although you have to handle it carefully to avoid damaging the color.

TITANIUM

Heavier than aluminum but lighter than steel, titanium is another material you can find as anodized jump rings. It is often used for medical implants, as it is hypoallergenic. Compared with niobium and aluminum, the surface of anodized titanium is more resistant to marring; however, you still need to be careful as you work. Titanium can be both the hardest and the most fragile material you work with. It can harden to such an extent that it breaks in half.

Working with Jump Rings

Working with jump rings is very straightforward. Simply close the jaws of two pairs of pliers on opposite sides of a jump ring, and twist the ring either open or closed. However, actually placing jump rings into a pattern can be somewhat trickier, especially if the pattern involves placing beads on the rings.

Here are some basic points to remember as you work:

○ You want to close the ring as tightly and evenly as possible. The best way to ensure good closures is to hold as much of the jump ring as possible in the pliers so that the pressure you apply is even. You also want to apply a small amount of cross-pressure as you bring the ends of a jump ring together. Some chain makers work the ends of a jump ring past each other with a small click in order to ensure a tight closure.

○ Never pull the ends of a jump ring apart to open it; this action pretty much ruins your chances of ever again closing the ring correctly. Always apply a twisting motion to open and close jump rings.

○ You want closed jump rings to be as flat as possible. Apply as equal a force as possible with both hands. If you tend to favor one hand over the other, you can end up with slightly distorted rings.

○ Do not force rings into place, especially through beads. This can often distort the shape of rings made from softer materials.

○ Applying the right amount of grip and force is important to ensure that you do not leave tool marks on the rings. Use smooth jaw or smooth tip pliers—or pliers with a coated tip—to work with soft materials. If you have trouble with tool marks, try using slightly larger pliers, which allow you to apply increased leverage with a lighter grip.

○ Never overwork your hands. The process of making chains tends to be highly repetitive. Take a lot of breaks; if your hands are sore, stop for the day. Fatigue can be a real issue, especially when working with the more delicate materials that are easily damaged when you can't apply your full strength to the project at hand.

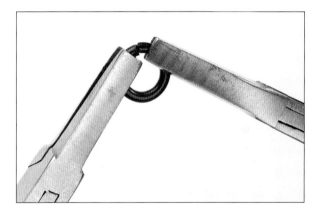

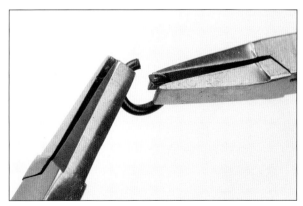

Jump Ring Illustrations

The projects in this book, and basic weaves described later in this Basics section, are accompanied by many (many!) illustrations. AN IMPORTANT THING TO KNOW: The colors in the illustrations are not meant to be the same as the actual rings used in the project. Instead, the colors tell you which are the rings you are working with in that individual step. The jump rings in the illustrations have been color coded as follows:

Red Rings: These are the open jump rings you are adding to the pattern during the project step in question. They always pass through silver rings and may or may not have blue rings on them.

Blue Rings: These are the pre-closed jump rings you are adding to the pattern during the project step. You always add them to red rings.

Silver Rings: These jump rings are part of the existing pattern and are involved in the project step. The red rings you add to the pattern always pass through silver rings. It is often important to note the way red rings pass through silver rings in order to construct the patterns correctly.

Black Rings: These jump rings are part of the existing pattern but are not involved in the project step. They are simply shown for reference purposes.

FIGURE 3

Other additions—such as beads, bells, and clasps—are also illustrated in silver, blue, and black, depending on how they relate to the current project step.

BEADS

Almost since the dawn of mankind, people have used beads of all kinds for adornment and commerce. Glass, bone, resin, shell, metal, stone, ceramic—today there are literally thousands of different kinds of beads available. Not all, however, are suitable for chain weaves.

The most appropriate beads for chain weaves are those with large holes. For a jump ring to fit through a bead, the bead's hole must be large enough to accommodate not only the gauge thickness of the jump ring but also a certain proportion of the jump ring's diameter. For example, you may have trouble fitting a jump ring through a bead that is more than half the jump ring's diameter in thickness, unless the bead has a very large hole (figure 4).

When you hunt for beads, remember these ratios. A lot of beads designed for stringing have holes that are too small for chain weave, so it can often be a great discovery to locate just the right bead for a given project!

Like wires, beads may also have a gauge designation that can vary from manufacturer to manufacturer. These gauges are usually defined in the form of "#/0" on a reverse scale, so that a size 4/0 bead is much larger than a size 12/0 bead.

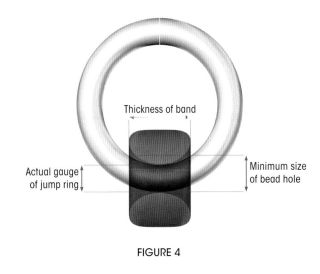

FIGURE 4

The shape of holes can vary widely as well, from round to square to totally irregular. Actually, square-holed beads can work well when threading jump rings through them.

It is important to pay attention to the bead's inner and outer coatings. Some exterior coatings are very fragile and can peel off if the beads are rubbed constantly, as they are in chain patterns. A bead's interior coating or lining can be just as fragile. Beads with metallic linings tend to be somewhat more stable and therefore more suitable for chain weaves.

DON'T GIVE UP

If at first you don't succeed, try again. This is an apt proverb when it comes to working with jump rings and beads. Bead manufacturing is not an exact science; the average container of beads has quite a variety of sizes, both of beads and bead holes. So you will often find beads in a container that simply won't work for your project. As a general rule of thumb, order three to four times as many beads as you think you will need for a project.

If you're having a really hard time getting a particular jump ring to fit through a particular batch of beads, try a jump ring with a slightly thinner gauge or slightly larger inner diameter (ID). A bead reamer (page 20) can also be an invaluable asset when it comes to stubborn beads.

Bead Varieties

The following is a list of the different kinds of beads especially well suited to chain weaves.

SEED BEADS

The smallest kind of glass bead, seed beads come in a variety of sizes, from 8/0 to 12/0, and are normally used for bead loom and weaving work, as well as for some embroidery. Most seed beads have rounded edges, but the ones with the most consistent sizing are often Japanese in origin and tend to have square ends.

Assorted small beads

In general, only the larger seed beads, such as size 8/0, are large enough to fit a jump ring. You may find a size 10/0 bead from a particular manufacturer that is suitable, but this is the exception rather than the rule. Size 12/0 seed beads are usually about 1 mm in diameter, 10/0 seed beads about 2 mm in diameter, and 8/0 seed beads about 3 mm in diameter.

"E" BEADS

Often categorized as size 6/0, these are the second smallest glass beads with rounded edges, next to seed beads. "E" beads come in a wide range of colors, linings, and finishes that, with the exception of more fragile faux metal finishes, are almost always suitable for chain weaves. "E" beads are approximately 4 mm in diameter.

"E" beads

PEBBLE BEADS

Following the same basic shape as seed and "E" beads, pebble beads are the next largest glass beads. They are often categorized as sizes 4/0 and 2/0. Pebble beads often come in the same range of colors as "E" beads and are almost always suitable for chain weaves. You'll find these beads most often have square holes. Size 4/0 pebble beads are about 5 mm in diameter, and size 2/0 pebble beads are about 6 mm in diameter.

PONY AND CROW BEADS

Pony and crow beads

The names for these large glass beads are basically interchangeable, although pony beads should have a slightly smaller diameter than crow beads: approximately 7 mm for pony beads and approximately 8 to 9 mm for crow beads. Pony beads are also more likely to have rounded edges, whereas crow beads often have square edges. Both of these beads are very suitable for chain weaves. While they do not have the same broad range of colors as other beads, you can find quite a wide selection when it comes to cheap, plastic pony and crow beads. Use these for less expensive jewelry projects.

ROLLER BEADS

These square-edged glass beads are basically miniature crow beads. They are often suitable for projects that require two sizes of identically colored and shaped beads. Roller beads are almost always 6 mm in diameter and tend to come in slightly more colors than crow beads.

Roller beads

WHITE HEART BEADS

These bi-color glass beads consist of a layer of opaque white glass covered by a layer of transparent glass that is often a true primary or secondary color. The white glass hearts of these beads often accentuate the transparent color to form bright, attractive beads. White hearts are most often found in 5 mm and 8 mm sizes, and both are usually fine to include in chain weaves.

STONE BEADS

Often available in sizes ranging from 1 mm to 10 mm and larger, stone beads usually have holes too small for most chain weaves. You can, however, use larger stone beads and other stone pendant shapes—such as donuts, triangles, and trapezoids—by wrapping them with chains, such as with the Bronze Age Bolo Tie on page 116.

PRECIOUS METAL SEAMLESS BEADS

Bright and attractive, these round sterling silver and gold-filled beads are some of the most consistent beads available to chain makers. Available in sizes from 1 to 8 mm, these beads are almost always perfect for chain weaves. Be careful with the larger sizes (6 to 8 mm), as the holes might be a little too small. Test a few before you buy a large quantity of these often-expensive beads.

DONUT BEADS

While larger beads suitable for chain weaves are often difficult to find, donut beads are the one exception to this rule. Normally measuring anywhere from 10 to 14 mm in diameter, donut beads can be made of glass and so come in a wide range of transparent and opaque colors, including some dazzling color combinations. Donut beads can also be made of stone (see photo). Look for donuts that have a larger-than-normal hole (3 to 4 mm).

LARGE FOCAL BEADS

You can also get large specialty beads from lampworkers (craftspeople who melt and shape glass). In fact, they are often delighted to tackle the challenge of creating custom focal beads. Color and design possibilities are only limited by your imagination; bead shows are often a wonderful source of inspiration! Be sure to show them the size of the jump ring you want to fit through the bead, and be aware that handmade beads often come with a certain amount of bead release in the hole, which you need to remove before using the bead.

Focal beads

If you have trouble with large holes, consider options for wrapping large custom focal beads. Alternatively, look for a different hole style, such as a glass pendant with a folded loop.

6 Place and close a new open large ring
through both a new closed small ring and
the small ring indicated in figure 59, which
was added as a closed ring as part of step
3. Be sure to keep the ring arrangement
from steps 4 and 5 intact.

FIGURE 59

7 Repeat step 6 until the chain reaches the
desired length.

DESIGN TIP
When weaving this pattern, the chain
always ends with a loose small jump ring.
In order to end the pattern evenly, either
remove the loose small jump ring or don't
add the small closed jump ring during the
final repetition of step 6.

The Projects

Early Frost
Necklace

This long Single Spiral chain uses glass roller beads to evoke the chilly splendor of a frosty day.

Finished Size Approximately 24 inches (61 cm)

MATERIALS

220 sterling silver jump rings, 16 gauge, $^7/_{32}$-inch ID (A)

55 crystal glass roller beads, 6 mm (B)

55 aquamarine lustre glass roller beads, 6 mm (C)

55 green lustre glass roller beads, 6 mm (D)

55 topaz lustre glass roller beads, 6 mm (E)

INSTRUCTIONS

1 Open all 220 jump rings (A).

2 Following the basic directions for adding beads to a Single Spiral chain on page 26, create a length of beaded spiral chain that consists of a total of 218 jump rings, with beads added to the chain in the pattern of (B), (C), (D), (E), repeated 54 times, followed by (B) and (C) once.

3 Place and close an open jump ring through the final two closed jump rings of one end of the chain, the final closed jump ring of the other end of the chain, and a roller bead (D), being sure to follow the correct twist of the chain and correct bead placement, as shown in figure 1.

FIGURE 1

4 Place and close an open jump ring through both the four closed jump rings shown and a glass roller bead (E), being sure to follow the correct twist of the chain and correct bead placement, as shown in figure 2.

FIGURE 2

DESIGN TIP
Note that due to the placement of the beads on the spiral, the final jump ring can be difficult to add correctly, so patience is advised as you complete this chain.

41

Circle Drop
Chandeliers

These whimsical earrings made from Double Cable chains are sure to excite and delight.

Finished Size Approximately 2¼ inches (5.7 cm) long

MATERIALS

98 spring hard sterling silver jump rings, 21 gauge, $^{15}/_{64}$-inch ID (A)

12 sterling silver jump rings, 21 gauge, $^{1}/_{8}$-inch ID (B)

16 sterling silver jump rings, 18 gauge, $^{5}/_{32}$-inch ID (C)

6 blue or red glass ring beads, 9 mm

2 surgical stainless steel 4-mm ball posts with loops and butterfly nuts

INSTRUCTIONS

1   Open 58 of the jump rings (A) and 14 of the jump rings (C). Close the other 40 jump rings (A), all 12 jump rings (B), and the last two jump rings (C).

2   Following the instructions on page 24, create a length of Double Cable chain that consists of 14 jump rings (A) and is seven jump ring (A) pairs in length.

3   One at a time, place and close two open jump rings (A) through both the final two jump rings (A) of the chain created in step 2 and two new closed jump rings (B).

4   One at a time, place and close two open jump rings (C) through both the two closed jump rings (B) from one end of the chain and a ring bead. Set this chain aside.

5   Repeat steps 2 and 3 to create a second chain.

6   One at a time, place and close two open jump rings (A) through both the two closed jump rings (B) from one end of the chain created in step 5 and a closed jump ring (C).

7   One at a time, place and close two open jump rings (A) through both the closed jump ring (C) added in step 6 and two new closed jump rings (A).

8   One at a time, place and close two open jump rings (C) through both the two closed jump rings (A) added in step 7 and a ring bead.

9   One at a time, place and close two open jump rings (A) through both the closed jump ring (C) added in step 6 and two new closed jump rings (A).

10 One at a time, place and close two open jump rings (A) through both the two closed jump rings (A) added in step 9 and two new closed jump rings (B).

11 One at a time, place and close two open jump rings (C) through both the two closed jump rings (B) added in step 10 and a ring bead.

12 One at a time, place and close two new open jump rings (A) through the final two jump rings (A) from the end of the chain opposite to what was added in steps 5 through 11.

13 Repeat step 12 on the opposite end of the chain, which was set aside after step 4.

14 Place and close an open jump ring (C) through the four jump rings (A) added in steps 12 and 13, which includes two jump rings (A) from the end of each chain, noting the position of the ring beads by referring to the photograph of this project.

15 Place and close an open jump ring (A) through both the jump ring (C) added in step 14 and the loop of a ball post.

16 Repeat steps 2 through 15, making sure to reverse the position of the glass rings beads during step 14, to create a second mirrored earring.

Beaded Persian Star Necklace

Connection Quartet

Beaded Persian Star Necklace

With the simple addition of a few glass beads, you can transform a cocktail necklace from a plain chain into an elegant piece of jewelry.

Finished Size Approximately 19 inches (48.3 cm) in circumference

MATERIALS

16-gauge sterling silver jump rings, as follows:

- ○ 76 with a $\frac{9}{32}$-inch ID (A)
- ○ 83 with an $\frac{11}{64}$-inch ID (B)
- ○ 7 with a $\frac{7}{32}$-inch ID (C)

38 silver-lined, square-holed, light amethyst glass beads, size 2/0

Sterling silver infinity clasp, 13 x 7 mm

INSTRUCTIONS

Preparing the Jump Rings

1 Open 38 of the large jump rings (A), 75 of the small jump rings (B), and four of the medium jump rings (C). Close the 38 other large jump rings (A) and the three other medium jump rings (C).

2 One at a time, place and close the 38 open large jump rings (A) through the 38 beads.

Creating the Chain

3 Following the instructions for making a Persian Star pattern chain (page 36), create a length of chain that consists of the 38 large jump rings (A) with the beads attached, 37 other large jump rings (A) without beads, and the 75 small jump rings (B). As you construct the Persian Star chain, ensure that all of the square-holed glass beads sit on the same side of the chain, as in figure 1.

FIGURE 1

DESIGN TIP
Add the large jump rings (A) to the Persian Star chain in an alternating fashion, with and without beads. You start and end with jump rings that have attached beads on the full length of the chain.

Finishing the Necklace

4 Following the instructions for creating cable pattern chains (page 23), construct a short adjustment chain from three medium jump rings (C), one large jump ring (A), and eight small jump rings (B) in four sets of two rings each, as shown in figure 2.

FIGURE 2

5 Place and close an open medium jump ring (C) through both a small jump ring (B) at one end of the Persian Star chain and the two small jump rings (B) at one end of the short adjustment chain.

6 Repeat step 5, placing and closing a second open medium jump ring (C) through both the same small jump ring (B) on the Persian Star chain and the same two small jump rings (B) on the short adjustment chain. Before you close the ring, however, make sure the large jump ring (A) with a bead on the end of the Persian Star chain is pinned between the new medium jump ring (B) and the one you added in step 5, as in figure 3.

FIGURE 3

7 Place and close an open medium jump ring (C) through both the small jump ring (B) at one end of the Persian Star chain and the loop of the silver clasp.

8 To complete the necklace, repeat step 7, placing and closing a second open medium jump ring (C) through both the same small jump ring (B) at one end of the Persian Star chain and the loop of the silver clasp. Before you close the ring, however, make sure the large jump ring (A) with a bead on the end of the Persian Star chain is pinned between the new medium jump ring (B) and the one you added in step 7, as in figure 4.

FIGURE 4

Connection Quartet

These bails, given here in four variations, are a fun and stylish way to attach pendants to necklaces and chains.

Byzantine Bail

Finished Size Bail: approximately 1 inch (2.5 cm) long

MATERIALS

16-gauge sterling silver jump rings, as follows:

○ 5 with an $^{11}/_{64}$-inch ID (A)

○ 2 with a $^{7}/_{32}$-inch ID (B)

○ 2 with a $^{9}/_{32}$-inch ID (C)

Sterling silver dragon pendant, 48 mm

18-inch (45.7 cm) length of ball chain, 2 mm

Ball chain clasp, 2 mm

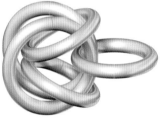

INSTRUCTIONS

1 Open one of the jump rings (A), both jump rings (B), and both jump rings (C). Close the four other jump rings (A).

2 Place and close an open jump ring (A) through the loop of the dragon pendant.

3 Place and close an open jump ring (B) through two new closed jump rings (A) and the jump ring (A) from step 2.

4 Repeat step 3, placing and closing a new open jump ring (B) through the same three closed jump rings (A).

5 Fold the two closed jump rings (A) backward, as shown in figure 1.

FIGURE 1

6 One at a time, place and close two open jump rings (C) through both the two closed jump rings (A) folded back in the previous step and two new closed jump rings (A), as shown in figure 2.

FIGURE 2

7 Run the ball chain through the final two closed jump rings (A) added in step 6, and end with the ball chain clasp.

Möbius Knot Bail

Finished Size Bail: approximately ¾ inch (1.9 cm) long

MATERIALS

11 gold-filled jump rings, 16 gauge, ⁹⁄₃₂-inch ID

Round paua shell pendant, 38 mm

26 to 28 inches (66 to 71.1 cm) of black braided cotton cord, 2 mm

2 black porcelain double-lace adjuster beads, 2 mm

INSTRUCTIONS

1   Open 10 of the jump rings and close the last one. Tie a loop knot in the center of the cotton cord. The knot in the photograph is a True Lover's Knot, but Figure Eight Knots also work very well. Feed one end of the cotton cord through one hole on each of two adjuster beads, and tie a simple knot in the end of the cotton cord. Feed the other end of the cotton cord through the remaining holes in each of the two adjuster beads, but from the opposite direction, and tie a simple knot in the end of the cotton cord.

2   Place and close an open jump ring through a closed jump ring.

3   Place and close a new open jump ring through the two closed jump rings from step 2, ensuring that the rings follow the same twist, as shown in figure 3.

FIGURE 3

4   Place and close a new open jump ring through the three closed jump rings from step 3, ensuring that the rings continue to follow the same twist, as shown in figure 4.

FIGURE 4

5   Repeat step 4 a total of four more times, placing and closing each new open jump ring through all of the previous rings and ensuring that all of the rings continue to follow the same twist to complete the Möbius Knot.

6   Place and close a new open jump ring through both all eight rings of the Möbius Knot and the hole of the shell pendant.

7   One at a time, place and close two new open jump rings through both all eight rings of the Möbius Knot and the loop of the adjustable cotton cord prepared earlier.

Rings of Saturn Bail

Finished Size Bail: approximately
1 inch (2.5 cm) long

MATERIALS

18-gauge sterling silver jump rings, as
    follows:

    ○   7 with a $^5/_{32}$-inch ID (A)

    ○   3 with a $^{15}/_{64}$-inch ID (B)

"B.C. jade" Maori fishhook pendant
    (Hei Matua), 50 mm

26 to 28 inches (66 to 71.1 cm) of
    black braided cotton cord,
    1 mm thick

2 black porcelain double-lace
    adjuster beads, 1 mm

INSTRUCTIONS

1 Open four of the small jump rings (A) and
all three of the large jump rings (B). Close
the other three small jump rings (A). Tie a
loop knot in the center of the cotton cord;
the knot in the photograph is a Figure Eight
Knot. Feed one end of the cotton cord
through one hole on each of two adjuster
beads, and tie a simple knot in the end of
the cotton cord. Feed the other end of the
cotton cord through the remaining holes of
each of the two adjuster beads, but from
the opposite direction, and tie a simple
knot in the end of the cotton cord.

2 One at a time, place and close two open
small jump rings (A) through both the
loop of the adjustable braided cord and a
closed small jump ring (A).

3 Place and close a new open small
jump ring (A) through two new
closed jump rings (A) and the closed
small jump ring (A) added in step 2.

4 Repeat the previous step, placing and
closing a new open small jump ring
(A) through the same three small
jump rings.

5 Fold the two closed small jump rings
(A) added in step 3 backward, as
shown in figure 5.

FIGURE 5

6 Place and close an open large jump ring
(B) through the two closed small jump rings
(A) folded backward in the previous step, as
shown in figure 6.

FIGURE 6

7 Place and close a new open large jump ring (B) through the two closed small jump rings (A) that were added as closed small jump rings in step 3, so that it sits between the two closed small jump rings folded back in step 5 and the jump ring (B) added in the previous step, as shown in figure 7.

FIGURE 7

8 Place and close a new open large jump ring (B) diagonally through both the two large jump rings (B) added in steps 6 and 7, as shown in figure 8, and through the hole of the fishhook pendant.

FIGURE 8

Double Cable Bail

Finished Size Bail: approximately 1¼ inches (3.2 cm) long

MATERIALS

6 sterling silver jump rings, 18 gauge, ⁵/₃₂-inch ID (A)

16-gauge sterling silver jump rings, as follows:

- ○ 2 with a ⁹/₃₂-inch ID (B)
- ○ 3 with a ⁷/₃₂-inch ID (C)
- ○ 2 with an ¹¹/₆₄-inch ID (D)

"Moonlight" crystal leaf pendant, 26 mm

Magnetic steel cable choker, 1 mm, 16-inch (40.6 cm) length

INSTRUCTIONS

1 Open all six jump rings (A) and one of the jump rings (C). Close both jump rings (B), the other two jump rings (C), and both jump rings (D).

2 Following the basic instructions for Double Cable chains on page 24, create a length of Double Cable chain that consists of two pairs of jump rings (B) connected to two pairs of jump rings (C), which are connected to two pairs of jump rings (D) by two pairs of jump rings (A) (figure 9).

FIGURE 9

3 Place and close an open jump ring (C) through both the hole of a crystal leaf pendant and the two closed jump rings (D) from one end of the Double Cable chain created in step 2. Close the jump ring.

4 One at a time, place and close two open jump rings (A) through the two closed jump rings (B) from the other end of the Double Cable chain and over the cable of the choker so that the cable choker passes through the jump rings (A) when they are closed.

Gypsy Cuff
Earrings

Tired of your regular earrings? Try something with a splash of sexy color and rakish style!

Finished Size Approximately 2 1/2 inches (6.4 cm) long

MATERIALS

21-gauge sterling silver jump rings, as follows:

- 120 with a 3/32-inch ID (A)
- 24 with a 1/8-inch ID (B)

2 sterling silver jump rings, 16 gauge, 7/32-inch ID (C)

Pair of plain sterling silver ear cuffs, 3 mm (D)

48 amethyst glass seed beads, size 8/0 (E)

2 amethyst translucent crow beads, 9 mm (F)

2 surgical stainless steel 4-mm ball posts with loop and butterfly nut

INSTRUCTIONS

1 Open 30 of the jump rings (A), all 12 jump rings (B), and the one jump ring (C). Close the other 30 jump rings (A).

2 Following the instructions on page 24, create a length of Double Cable chain that consists of 29 jump ring (A) pairs.

3 Place and close an open jump ring (A) through both the final pair of closed jump rings (A) from one end of the Double Cable chain created in step 2 and the hole of an ear cuff (D).

4 Place and close an open jump ring (B) through both the jump ring (A) added in the previous step and two seed beads (E), as shown in figure 1.

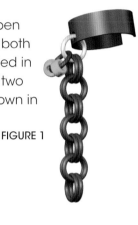

FIGURE 1

5 Repeat the previous step a total of 11 more times, placing and closing new jump rings (B) with two seed beads (E) onto the second, fourth, sixth, eighth, 10th, 12th, 14th, 16th, 18th, 20th, and 22nd pairs of jump rings (A) from the Double Cable chain. Ensure that the beads are on the "outside" of the Double Cable chain (figure 2).

FIGURE 2

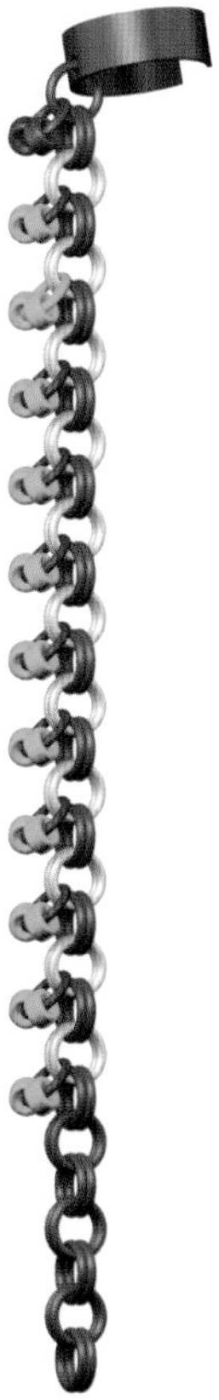

6 Place and close an open jump ring (A) through both the 25th jump ring (A) pair from the Double Cable chain and the loop of a ball post. Ensure that the ball post is attached to the "inside" of the Double Cable chain, with the post facing "backwards," as shown in figure 3.

FIGURE 3

7 Place and close an open jump ring (C) through both the final jump ring (A) pair from the Double Cable chain and a crow bead (F).

8 To create the left ear cuff, repeat steps 2 through 7 and reverse the direction of the ball post.

Mermaid's Tail

Delicate and sassy, these little earrings demand attention with a splash of fine color.

Finished Size Approximately 1½ inches (3.8 cm) long)

MATERIALS

2 sterling silver jump rings, 16 gauge, 9/32-inch ID (A)

66 spring hard sterling silver jump rings, 21 gauge, 3/32-inch ID (B)

14 emerald glass seed beads, size 8/0

2 surgical stainless steel 4-mm ball posts with loops and butterfly nuts

INSTRUCTIONS

1 Open both large jump rings (A) and 40 of the small jump rings (B). Close the other 26 small jump rings (B).

2 Following the basic instructions for creating Double Cable pattern chains on page 24, construct a short length of Double Cable chain from four closed small jump rings (B) and two open small jump rings (B). Set this chain aside.

3 Place and close an open large jump ring (A) through nine small closed jump rings (B).

4 Following the instructions for the basic European 1 in 4 pattern on page 28, use the nine small closed jump rings (B) added in the previous step and eight new open small jump rings (B) as the base to create a new row consisting of eight small jump rings (B).

5 Continuing to follow the instructions for the basic European 1 in 4 pattern on page 28, use the eight small closed jump rings (B) added in the previous step and seven new open small jump rings (B) as the base to create a new row consisting of seven small jump rings (B). As each of the seven new open small jump rings (B) are added, place each ring through one seed bead (figure 1).

FIGURE 1

6 Place and close an open small jump ring (B) through both the large closed jump ring (A) and two closed small jump rings (B) from the end of the short length of Double Cable chain prepared in step 2.

7 Repeat the previous step, placing and closing a second open small jump ring (B) through both the same large closed jump ring (A) and the same two closed small jump rings (B) from the end of the short length of Double Cable chain prepared in step 2.

8 Finish the earring by placing and closing a small open jump ring (B) through both the two small closed jump rings (B) at the opposite end of the short length of Double Cable chain and the loop of a ball post (figure 2).

FIGURE 2

9 To create the second earring as a mirror image of the first, follow steps 2 through 8, except that base rows of small closed jump rings (B) attached in step 3 should overlap in the opposite direction of the base rows of the first earring.

Bejewelled
Eyeglass Chain

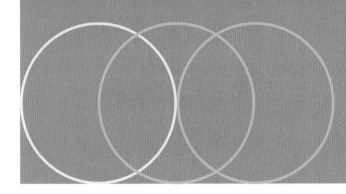

Here's a lightweight aluminum eyeglass chain for the hip librarian in your life!

Finished Size Approximately 24 inches (61 cm) long

MATERIALS

214 bright aluminum jump rings, 18 gauge, $7/32$-inch ID (A)

50 amethyst glass "E" beads, size 6/0 (B)

25 "hyacinth ghost" glass "E" beads, size 6/0 (C)

25 "crystal ghost" glass "E" beads, size 6/0 (D)

2 clear eyeglass holders

INSTRUCTIONS

1 Open all 214 jump rings (A).

2 Following the basic directions for adding beads to a Single Spiral chain on page 26, create a length of beaded spiral chain that consists of a total of 202 jump rings with beads added to the chain in the pattern of:

○ Jump ring with "E" bead (B)
○ Jump ring with no bead
○ Jump ring with "E" bead (C)
○ Jump ring with no bead
○ Jump ring with "E" bead (B)
○ Jump ring with no bead
○ Jump ring with "E" bead (D)

Repeated 25 times, followed by:
○ Jump ring with no bead
○ Jump ring with "E" bead (C)
○ Jump ring with no bead
○ Jump ring with "E" bead (B)

This creates a beaded Single Spiral chain with beads on every second link.

3 Following the basic directions for the Single Spiral chain on page 24, add three more open jump rings (A) with no beads to one end of the chain created in step 2.

4 Place and close an open jump ring (A) through both the final two closed jump links (A) added in step 3 and the loop of an eyeglass holder, making sure to follow the correct twist of the spiral pattern.

5 Place and close an open jump ring (A) through the final closed jump link (A) added in step 3, the closed jump link (A) added in step 4, and the loop of an eyeglass holder, making sure to follow the correct twist of the spiral pattern as shown in figure 1.

FIGURE 1

6 Repeat steps 3 through 5 to complete the other end of the chain.

61

Moroccan Double Spiral Bracelet

Glass ring beads add an extra dimension of translucent color to an ordinary chain mail pattern in this exotic bracelet.

Finished Size Approximately 8½ inches (21.6 cm) in circumference

MATERIALS

18-gauge copper jump rings, as follows:

- ○ 30 with a ¼-inch ID (A)
- ○ 64 with a ⁷⁄₃₂-inch ID (B)
- ○ 7 with a ⅛-inch ID (C)

8 ruby glass ring beads, 9 mm

Copper-plated lobster claw clasp, 12 x 6.4 mm

INSTRUCTIONS

1 Open all 30 jump rings (A), 61 of the jump rings (B), and all seven jump rings (C). Close the three remaining jump rings (B).

2 One at a time, place and close two open jump rings (A) through a ring bead.

3 One at a time, place and close two open jump rings (B) through the two jump rings (A) added in step 2.

4 Following the basic instructions for creating a Double Spiral pattern chain on page 26, use the two jump rings (A) added in step 2 and the two jump rings (B) added in step 3 as the base to add six more open jump rings (B) following the Double Spiral pattern, as shown in figure 1.

FIGURE 1

5 One at a time, place and close two open jump rings (A) through both the four jump rings (B) from the end of the Double Spiral chain created in step 4 (following the direction of the spiral) and a new ring bead.

FIGURE 2

6 Create a continuous chain by repeating steps 2 through 5 a total of six more times, except that the ring bead added in step 5 is the ring bead started with when repeating step 2.

7 Repeat steps 2 and 3 once more, except that the ring bead started with in step 2 is one of the ring beads from the end of the chain.

8 Place and close an open jump ring (B), following the spiral of the chain, through both the two jump rings (A) and two jump rings (B) added in the previous step.

9 Place and close an open jump ring (C), following the spiral of the chain, through the two jump rings (B) added in step 7, through the two jump rings (B) added in the previous step, and the loop of a clasp (figure 3).

FIGURE 3

10 Following the basic instructions for creating cable pattern chains on page 23, construct a short adjustment chain from three closed jump rings (B) and six jump rings (C) in three sets of two rings each, one set loose at the end of the chain.

11 Finish the bracelet by placing and closing an open jump ring (B) through both the ring bead from the opposite end of the chain and the two jump rings (B) at the end of the small adjustment chain created in the previous step (figure 4).

FIGURE 4

Drops of Jupiter

> This jaw-dropping necklace features hand-made beads with specks of real gold mined from the Canadian Yukon and expertly frozen into dazzling glass.

Finished Size Approximately 18 inches (45.7 cm) in circumference

MATERIALS

16-gauge gold-filled jump rings, as follows:

- 58 with a $\frac{9}{32}$-inch ID (A)
- 282 with an $\frac{11}{64}$-inch ID (B)

12 gold-filled jump rings, 18 gauge, $\frac{5}{32}$-inch ID (C)

6 donut beads, 10 to 12 mm

Gold-plated lobster claw clasp, 13 mm

INSTRUCTIONS

1. Open 56 of the jump rings (A), 172 of the jump rings (B), and all 12 jump rings (C). Close the last two jump rings (A) and the other 110 jump rings (B).

2. Place and close a jump ring (A) through a donut bead. Repeat with the five remaining donut beads.

3. Following the instructions for Byzantine chain on page 30, construct a length Byzantine pattern chain that consists of a total of 50 jump rings (A) in pairs and 240 jump rings (B).

DESIGN TIP
Make sure that you use jump rings (A) as the large jump rings in steps 2, 10, and 11 of the base Byzantine chain pattern. Use jump rings (B) in place of the large jump rings added in steps 5, 6, 15, and 16 of the base Byzantine chain pattern.

4. Temporarily mark the seventh, 10th, 13th, 16th, and 19th jump ring (A) pairs from the Byzantine chain created in step 3.

5. One at a time, place and close two open jump rings (B) through both a jump ring (A) with a donut bead created in step 2 and two closed jump rings (B).

6. Fold the closed jump rings (B) added in step 5 backward, as in the base Byzantine chain pattern.

7. One at a time, place and close two open jump rings (B) through both the closed jump rings (B) that were added in step 5 and the seventh pair of jump rings (A) from the Byzantine chain created in step 3 (figure 1).

FIGURE 1

8 Repeat step 7 a total of three more times, adding jump rings (A) with donut beads to the 10th, 16th, and 17th jump ring (A) pairs from the Byzantine chain created in step 3, making sure that all the beads added are on the same side of the chain.

9 Following the instructions for Byzantine chain on page 30 and using a jump ring (A) with donut bead created in step 2 as a base, create a short length of Byzantine chain that consists of the jump ring (A) with donut bead and 16 jump rings (B). This means that the Byzantine chain will not actually end correctly; you must fold it back before continuing on to step 10.

10 One at a time, place and close two open jump rings (B) through both the final closed jump rings (B) of the short length of Byzantine chain created in step 9 and the 13th pair of jump rings (A) from the Byzantine chain created in step 3 (figure 2).

FIGURE 2

11 Place and close an open jump ring (B) through the loop of the clasp.

12 One at a time, place and close two open jump rings (C) through both the final pair of jump rings (A) from one end of the main chain created in step 3 and the jump ring (B) added to the clasp in step 11.

13 One at a time, place and close two open jump rings (C) through both the final pair of jump rings (A) from the other end of the main chain created in step 3 and a closed jump ring (B).

14 One at a time, place and close two open jump rings (C) through both the closed jump ring (B) added in step 13 and a closed jump ring (A).

15 Repeat steps 13 and 14 twice to create an adjustment chain. Use a closed jump ring (A) with a donut bead that was created in step 2 as the final closed jump ring.

Centipede
Bracelet & Earrings

This technique uses a size variation of the basic European 1 in 4 pattern to create an elegantly simple bracelet and earring set.

BASIC EUROPEAN 1 IN 4 VARIATION TECHNIQUE

This pattern requires at least two sizes of jump rings. Open all the jump rings required for the project, large and small.

1 Place and close all of the large jump rings required for the project through beads appropriate to their dimensions (see below for specific size information), as shown in figure 1.

FIGURE 1

2 Place and close an open small jump ring through two of the larger jump rings with beads prepared in step 1, as shown in figure 2.

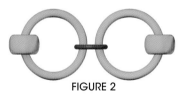
FIGURE 2

3 Repeat step 2, placing and closing a second open small jump ring through the same two large jump rings with beads prepared in step 1, as shown in figure 3.

FIGURE 3

4 Fold the large jump ring with a bead added in step 2 backward, as shown in figure 4, to create the start of the centipede pattern chain.

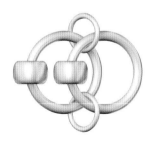
FIGURE 4

5 Place and close an open small jump ring through one of the large jump rings with a bead prepared in step 1 and the large jump ring with a bead at the end of the centipede pattern chain, as shown in figure 5.

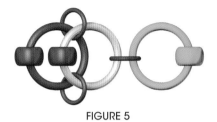

FIGURE 5

6 Repeat the previous step, placing and closing an open small jump ring through the same large jump ring with a bead prepared in step 1 and the large jump ring with a bead from the end of the centipede pattern, as shown in figure 6.

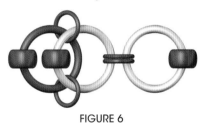

FIGURE 6

7 Fold the large jump ring with a bead added in step 5 backward, as shown in figure 7, to continue the centipede pattern chain.

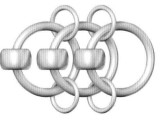

FIGURE 7

8 Continue the process of adding new large jump rings with beads, as in steps 5, 6, and 7, until the centipede pattern chain is complete.

Bracelet

Finished Size Fits a 8½-inch (21.6 cm) diameter wrist, approximately

MATERIALS

32 seamless sterling silver beads, 5 mm

16-gauge sterling silver jump rings, as follows:

- 32 with a ⁹⁄₃₂-inch ID (A)
- 2 with a ⁷⁄₃₂-inch ID (B)
- 3 with an ¹¹⁄₆₄-inch ID (C)

72 spring hard sterling silver jump rings, 21 gauge, ⅛-inch ID (D)

1 sterling silver infinity clasp, 13 x 7 mm

INSTRUCTIONS

1 Open all 32 jump rings (A), one of the jump rings (B), and all 72 jump rings (D). Close the other jump ring (B) and all three jump rings (C).

2 Place and close a jump ring (A) through a seamless bead. Repeat with the remaining 31 seamless beads.

3 Using the prepared jump rings (A) with seamless beads from step 2 and 64 of the open jump rings (D), follow steps 2 through 8 of the Basic European 1 in 4 Variation Technique to create a centipede chain that is 32 closed jump rings with beads in length.

4 Place and close the open jump ring (B) through the loop of the clasp.

5 Place and close an open jump ring (D) through both the closed jump ring (A) with a seamless bead from the end of the centipede chain, where the seamless bead faces out, and the closed jump ring (B) with clasp prepared in step 4 (figure 8).

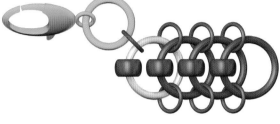

FIGURE 8

6 Fold the closed jump ring (B) with the lobster claw clasp into the position shown in figure 9.

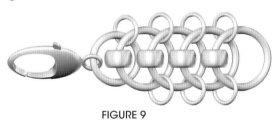

FIGURE 9

7 Repeat step 5, placing and closing a second open jump ring (D) through the same closed jump ring (A) with a seamless bead from the end of the centipede chain, where the seamless bead faces out, and through the closed jump ring (B) with a clasp added in step 5 (figure 10).

FIGURE 10

8 Place and close an open jump ring (D) through the closed jump ring (A) with a seamless bead from the end of the centipede chain, where the seamless bead does not face out, and the closed jump ring (B) (figure 11).

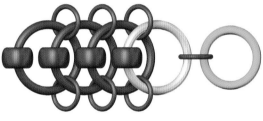

FIGURE 11

9 Repeat step 8, placing and closing a second open jump ring (D) through both the same closed jump ring (A) with a bead from the end of the centipede chain, where the seamless bead does not face out, and the closed jump ring (B) added in the previous step, folding the closed jump ring (B) in to the position shown in figure 12.

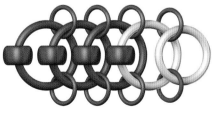

FIGURE 12

10 Create a short adjustment chain to finish the bracelet, by placing and closing six open jump rings (D) through both the three closed jump rings (C) and the closed jump ring (B) added in step 8, as shown in figure 13.

FIGURE 13

Earrings

Finished Size Approximately 1¼ inch (3.2 cm)

MATERIALS

10 sterling silver jump rings, 18 gauge, ¹⁵⁄₆₄-inch ID (A)

18 spring hard sterling silver jump rings, 21 gauge, ³⁄₃₂-inch ID (B)

10 seamless sterling silver beads, 4 mm

2 surgical stainless steel 4-mm ball posts with loops and butterfly nuts

INSTRUCTIONS

1 Open all 10 jump rings (A) and all 18 jump rings (B).

2 Place and close a jump ring (A) through a seamless bead. Repeat with four more seamless beads.

3 Using the prepared jump rings with beads from step 2 and eight open jump rings (B), follow steps 2 through 8 of the Basic European 1 in 4 Variation Techique on page 69 to create a centipede chain that is five closed jump rings with beads in length.

4 Place and close an open jump ring (B) through both the closed jump ring (A) with a bead from the end of the centipede chain that doesn't have a bead, created in step 2, and the loop of a surgical stainless steel ball post (figure 14).

5 Repeat steps 2 through 4 to create a second identical earring.

FIGURE 14

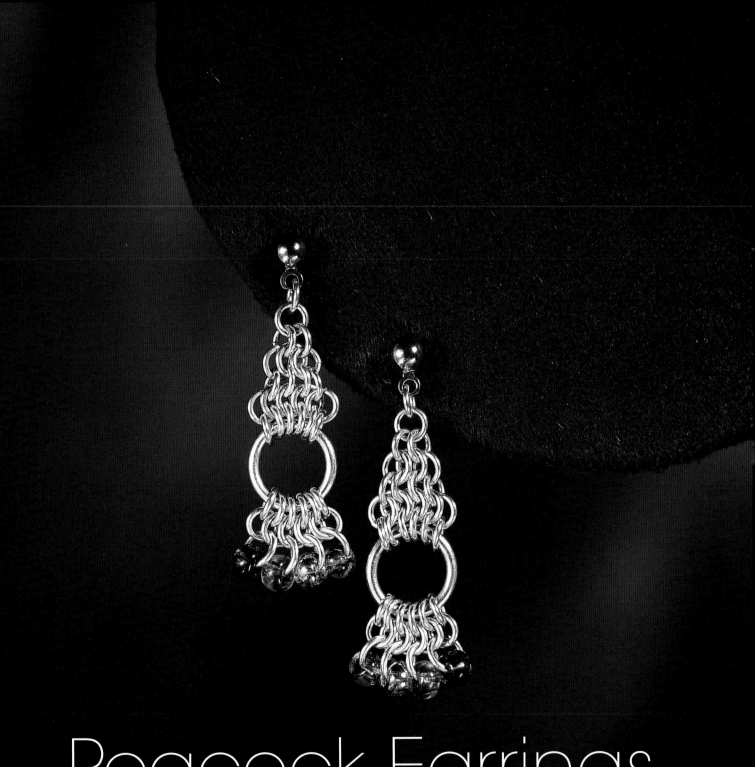

Peacock Earrings

Employ the basic European 1 in 4 Pattern and four shades of blue and green beads to create earrings inspired by the fan of a peacock's tail.

Finished Size Approximately 1 inch (2.5 cm) long

MATERIALS

2 sterling silver jump rings, 16 gauge, ⁹⁄₃₂-inch ID (A)

66 spring hard sterling silver jump rings, 21 gauge, ³⁄₃₂-inch ID (B)

8 sterling silver jump rings, 21 gauge, ¹⁄₈-inch ID (C)

2 peridot lustre glass "E" beads, size 6/0 (D)

2 blue zircon glass "E" beads, size 6/0 (E)

2 teal translucent glass "E" beads, size 6/0 (F)

2 aquamarine glass "E" beads, size 6/0 (G)

2 surgical stainless steel 4-mm ball posts with loops and butterfly nuts

INSTRUCTIONS

1 Open both jump rings (A), 42 of the jump rings (B), and all eight jump rings (C). Close the other 24 jump rings (B).

2 Place and close an open large jump ring (A) through 12 small closed jump rings (B). Separate the small closed jump rings (B) into two groups consisting of six small closed jump rings (B) each.

3 Following the instructions for the basic European 1 in 4 pattern on page 28, use one group of six small closed jump rings (B) as the base for a triangle of European 1 in 4 pattern mail made from small jump rings (B). The triangle consists of a total of six rows; reduce the total number of jump rings (B) by one each row.

4 Use the other group of six small closed jump rings (B) as the base for a row of European 1 in 4 pattern mail that consists of five small closed jump rings (B), as shown in figure 1.

FIGURE 1

5 Place and close an open medium jump ring (C) through both the first two closed jump rings (B) from the row of five small closed jump rings (B) created in the last step and an "E" bead (E).

6 Repeat the process of the previous step, using three more open medium jump links (C) to attach the three remaining colors of glass "E" beads (D, F, and G) to the row of five small closed jump rings (B) created in step 4 (figure 2).

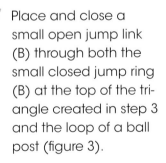

FIGURE 2

7 Place and close a small open jump link (B) through both the small closed jump ring (B) at the top of the triangle created in step 3 and the loop of a ball post (figure 3).

FIGURE 3

8 To create the second earring as a mirror image of the first, follow steps 2 through 7, except that base rows of small closed jump rings (B) attached in steps 3 and 4 should overlap in the opposite direction of the base rows of the first earring.

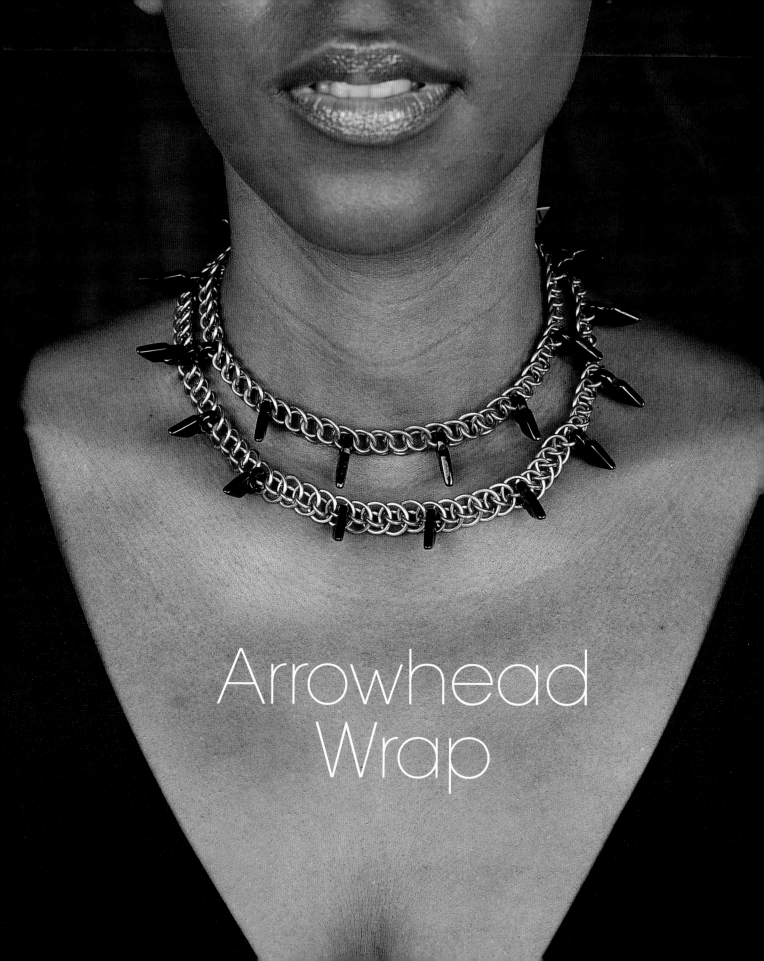

Arrowhead
Wrap

Here's something completely different. Spiky beads add a hip third dimension to this chain that you can wear as either a choker or a bracelet.

Finished Size Approximately 30 inches (76.2 cm) long

MATERIALS

16-gauge jewelry brass jump rings, as follows:

- 133 with $9/32$-inch ID (A)

- 133 with $11/64$-inch ID (B)

25 black, triangular glass hair pendant beads (aka *Talhakimt* or *Taunfaulk* beads), 18 mm

Sleeve-style magnetic clasp, 34 mm

INSTRUCTIONS

1 Open all 133 jump rings (A) and 29 of the jump rings (B). Close the other 104 jump rings (B).

2 One at a time, place and close 25 open jump rings (B) through one triangular bead each.

3 Following the instructions for Persian Star chain on page 36, construct a length of chain that consists of a total of 125 jump rings (A), 100 jump rings (B), and the 25 jump rings (B) with triangular beads created in step 2 (added to the regular Persian Star pattern as every fifth jump ring (B) of the pattern, with all the triangular beads on the same side of the chain).

4 One at a time, place and close two open jump rings (A) through both the final jump ring (B) of the chain, with one of the jump rings (A) added above, and the other jump ring (A) added below the final jump ring (A) of the chain, as shown in figure 1.

FIGURE 1

5 One at a time, place and close two open jump rings (B) through both the jump rings (A) added in step 4 and the loop from one side of the magnetic clasp.

6 Repeat steps 4 and 5 with the other end of the chain and the other side of the magnetic clasp.

Golden Lady Earrings

This spiralling method of adding beads transforms a Single Cable chain into something dazzling.

Finished Size Approximately 1½ inches (3.8 cm) long

MATERIALS

18 gold-filled jump rings, 18 gauge, ⁵/₃₂-inch ID (A)

18 seamless gold-filled beads, 4 mm (B)

2 14kt gold-filled French clips (C)

INSTRUCTIONS

1 Open all 18 jump rings (A).

2 Place and close an open jump ring (A) through a seamless bead (B).

3 Place and close a new open jump ring (A) through both a seamless bead (B) and the jump ring (A) from step 2.

4 Place and close a new open jump ring (A) through both a seamless bead (B) and the jump ring (A) added in step 3, making sure that the seamless bead (B) added in step 3 sits to the right of the chain, as shown in figure 1.

FIGURE 1

5 Place and close a new open jump ring (A) through both a seamless bead (B) and the jump ring (A) added in step 4, making sure that the seamless bead (B) added in step 4 sits to the top of the chain, as shown in figure 2.

FIGURE 2

6 Place and close a new open jump ring (A) through both a seamless bead (B) and the jump ring (A) added in step 5, making sure that the seamless bead (B) added in step 5 sits to the left of the chain, as shown in figure 3.

FIGURE 3

79

7 Place and close a new open jump ring (A) through both a seamless bead (B) and the jump ring (A) added in step 6, making sure that the seamless bead (B) added in step 6 sits to the bottom of the chain, as shown in figure 4.

FIGURE 4

8 Place and close a new open jump ring (A) through both a seamless bead (B) and the jump ring (A) added in step 7, making sure that the seam-less bead (B) added in step 7 sits to the right of the chain, as shown in figure 5.

FIGURE 5

9 Place and close a new open jump ring (A) through both a seamless bead (B) and the jump ring (A) added in step 8, making sure that the seam-less bead (B) added in step 8 sits to the top of the chain, as shown in figure 6.

FIGURE 6

10 Place and close a new open jump ring (A) through a seamless bead (B), the jump ring (A) added in step 9, and the loop of a French clip (C), making sure that the seamless bead (B) added in step 9 sits to the left of the chain and that the seamless bead (B) added during this step sits to the bottom of the chain, as shown in figure 7.

FIGURE 7

11 Repeat steps 2 through 10, being sure to spiral the beads in the opposite direction around the single cable chain to create the second earring.

Zigzag Bracelet

In this classy, flashy bracelet, the "X" patterns formed by the green beads dance back and forth along the Double Cable chain.

Finished Size Approximately 7½ inches (19 cm) in circumference

MATERIALS

132 sterling silver jump rings, 21 gauge,
⅛-inch ID (A)

7 sterling silver jump rings, 16 gauge,
9/32-inch ID (B)

18-gauge sterling silver jump rings, as follows:

○   56 with a ⅛-inch ID (C)

○   24 with a 5/32-inch ID (D)

28 green iris glass "E" beads

Sterling silver infinity clasp, 13 mm

INSTRUCTIONS

1   Open all 132 jump rings (A), all seven jump
rings (B), and two of the jump rings (D).
Close all 56 jump rings (C) and the other 22
jump rings (D).

2   One at a time, place and close a total of
seven open jump rings (B) through four "E"
beads each. Note that these jump rings (B)
can be slightly hard to close; patience is
advised as you add the "E" beads.

3   One at a time, place and close two open
jump rings (A) through two closed jump
rings (C) and two closed jump rings (D).

4   Repeat step 3 a total of three more times,
adding three more pairs of closed jump
rings (C) to the pair of closed jump rings (D)
from step 3 to create a small cross-shaped
piece of Double Cable chain, as shown in
figure 1.

FIGURE 1

5   Repeat steps 3 and 4 a total of five more
times to create a total of six small cross-
shaped pieces of Double Cable chain.

6   One at a time, place and close two open
jump rings (A) through both one of the
jump rings (B) with four "E" beads prepared
in step 2 and a pair of closed jump rings
(C) from one of the small cross-shaped
pieces of Double Cable chain created in
steps 4 and 5.

7 One at a time, place and close two open jump rings (A) through both the same jump ring (B) with four "E" beads as in step 6 and the next pair of closed jump rings (C) from the same small cross-shaped piece of Double Cable chain as in step 6. Make sure that the open jump rings (A) are added to the jump ring (B) at the next point between the "E" beads, as shown in figure 2.

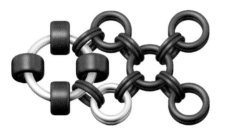

FIGURE 2

8 One at a time, place and close two open jump rings (A) through both a new jump ring (B) with four "E" beads prepared in step 2 and the next pair of closed jump rings (C) from the same small cross-shaped piece of Double Cable chain as in step 6.

9 One at a time, place and close two open jump rings (A) through both the same jump ring (B) with four "E" beads as step 8 and the final pair of closed jump rings (C) from the same small cross-shaped piece of Double Cable chain as in step 6. Make sure that the open jump rings (A) are added to the jump ring (B) at the next point between the "E" beads, as illustrated in figure 3.

FIGURE 3

10 Following the same process as steps 6 through 9, create a length of chain that includes all seven jump rings (B) with four "E" beads and all six small cross-shaped pieces of Double Cable chain.

11 One at a time, place and close two jump rings (A) through two of the jump ring (C) pairs from the first small cross-shaped piece of Double Cable chain, as illustrated in figure 4.

FIGURE 4

12 Repeat step 11 a total of five more times, once for each small cross-shaped piece of Double Cable chain remaining, making sure to alternate the side of the two jump ring (C) pairs joined, as in the photograph of the finished bracelet.

13 One at a time, place and close two open jump rings (D) through the loop of a clasp.

14 One at a time, place and close two open jump rings (A) through both the two closed jump rings (D) from step 13 and the closed jump ring (B) with four "E" beads from one end of the chain. Make sure that the open jump rings (A) are added to the jump ring (B) at the next point between the "E" beads.

15 One at a time, place and close two open jump rings (A) through both the two closed jump rings (D) from step 13 and the same closed jump ring (B) with four "E" beads from one end of the chain as in step 14. Make sure that the open jump rings (A) are added to the jump ring (B) at the next point between the "E" beads, as shown in figure 5.

FIGURE 5

16 Following the basic instructions for creating Double Cable chain on page 24, create a short length of Double Cable chain that consists of five pairs of jump rings (D) connected by four pairs of jump rings (A).

17 One at a time, place and close two open jump rings (A) through both two closed jump rings (D) from one end of the short Double Cable chain created in step 16 and the closed jump ring (B) with four "E" beads from the other end of the chain. Make sure that the open jump rings (A) are added to the jump ring (B) at the next point between the "E" beads.

18 One at a time, place and close two open jump rings (A) through both the two closed jump rings (D) from step 17 and the same closed jump ring (B) with four "E" beads from the other end of the chain as step 17. Make sure that the open jump rings (A) are added to the jump ring (B) at the next point between the "E" beads, as illustrated in figure 6.

FIGURE 6

Shell Spiral Earrings

Reminiscent of silver sea shells, these dazzling spirals will showcase your chain mail skills to impressive effect.

Finished Size Approximately 3 inches (7.6 cm) long

MATERIALS

20-gauge sterling silver jump rings, as follows:

- 6 with a $^7/_{64}$-inch ID (A)
- 12 with a $^1/_8$-inch ID (B)
- 12 with a $^3/_{16}$-inch ID (C)

18-gauge sterling silver jump rings, as follows:

- 12 with a $^3/_{16}$-inch ID (D)
- 12 with a $^7/_{32}$-inch ID (E)
- 6 with a $^1/_4$-inch ID (F)

12 seamless sterling silver beads, 2 mm (G)

12 seamless sterling silver beads, 3 mm (H)

12 seamless sterling silver beads, 4 mm (I)

12 seamless sterling silver beads, 5 mm (J)

6 seamless sterling silver beads, 6 mm (K)

2 surgical stainless steel 4-mm ball posts with loops and butterfly nuts

INSTRUCTIONS

1 Open all the jump rings required for this project.

2 Following the basic instructions for adding beads to a Single Spiral pattern chain on page 26, create a beaded Single Spiral pattern chain as follows:

- Two jump rings (A)
- Three jump rings (B), each with a seamless silver bead (G)
- Three jump rings (C), each with a seamless silver bead (H)
- Three jump rings (D), each with a seamless silver bead (I)
- Three jump rings (E), each with a seamless silver bead (J)
- Three jump rings (F), each with a seamless silver bead (K)
- Three jump rings (E), each with a seamless silver bead (J)
- Three jump rings (D), each with a seamless silver bead (I)
- Three jump rings (C), each with a seamless silver bead (H)
- Three jump rings (B), each with a seamless silver bead (G)

3 Complete the earring by placing and closing an open jump ring (A) through both the two closed jump rings (A) from one end of the beaded Single Spiral chain, following the direction of the spiral, and the loop of a ball post (figure 1).

FIGURE 1

4 To create the second earring that is a mirror image of the first, repeat steps 2 and 3, reversing the direction of the spiral, as explained in the Single Spiral chain pattern instructions on page 24.

Dancing Bells Anklet

A lightweight Persian Star chain melds effortlessly with flashy bells to create a melodic anklet, perfect for dancing away the day on a sun-soaked beach.

Finished Size Approximately 9½ inches (24.1 cm) in circumference

MATERIALS

18-gauge stainless steel jump rings, as follows:

- 40 with a ¼-inch ID (A)
- 7 with a ³/₁₆-inch ID (B)
- 49 with a ⁵/₃₂-inch ID (C)

39 stainless steel jump rings, 20 gauge, ⁵/₃₂-inch ID (D)

39 silver-plated bells, 6 mm

Stainless steel lobster clasp, 15 mm

INSTRUCTIONS

1 Close all 40 jump rings (A), four of the jump rings (B), 47 of the jump rings (C), and all 39 jump rings (D). Close the other three jump rings (B) and the last two jump rings (C).

2 Following the basic instructions for creating a Persian Star pattern chain on page 36, create a length of Persian Star chain that consists of 40 jump rings (A) and 40 jump rings (B).

3 Following the basic instructions for creating Cable pattern chains on page 23, construct a short adjustment chain from three closed jump rings (B) and six jump rings (C) in three sets of two jump rings each, one set loose at the end of the chain, as shown in figure 1.

FIGURE 1

4 Place and close an open jump ring (D) through both two closed jump rings (A) from one end of the Persian Star chain and a plated bell, as shown in figure 2.

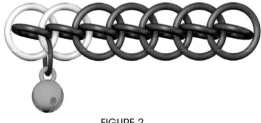

FIGURE 2

89

5 Continue adding the remaining 38 plated bells to the Persian Star chain, attaching each to the chain using an open jump ring (D) that has been placed through two closed jump rings (A) from one side of the chain and closed, as shown in figure 3.

FIGURE 3

DESIGN TIP

With the exception of the first closed jump ring (A) from each end of the Persian Star chain, each closed jump ring (A) should have a total of two plated bells attached to it.

6 Place and close an open jump ring (B) through both the closed jump ring (C) from one end of the Persian Star chain and the two closed jump rings (C) from the end of the short adjustment chain prepared earlier.

7 Repeat the previous step, placing and closing a second open jump ring (B) through both the same closed jump ring (C) from one end of the Persian Star chain and the same two closed jump rings (C) from the end of the short adjustment chain. However, add this ring on the opposite side of the closed jump ring (A) from the same end of the Persian Star chain, pinning that jump ring (A) between the jump rings (B) added in this step and in the previous step, as shown in figure 4.

FIGURE 4

8 Place and close an open jump ring (B) through both the closed jump ring (C) from the opposite end of the Persian Star chain and two new closed jump rings (C).

9 Repeat the previous step, placing and closing a second open jump ring (B) through both the same closed jump ring (C) from the end of the Persian Star chain and the same two closed jump rings (C). However, add this ring on the opposite side of the closed jump ring (A) from the same end of the Persian Star chain, pinning that jump ring (A) between the jump rings (B) added in this step and the previous step.

10 Complete the anklet by placing and closing an open jump ring (B) through both the two closed jump rings (C) added in step 8 and the loop of a clasp (figure 5).

FIGURE 5

Chain Gang

The simple cable chain variation used here is perfect for creating a rugged yet stylish set of wallet, boot, and key chains.

CHAIN GANG VARIATION INSTRUCTIONS

1 Open all the jump rings required for the project.

2 Place and close an open stainless steel jump ring (A) through a barrel bead (figure 1).

FIGURE 1

3 Place and close an open bronze jump ring (B) through the same barrel bead as step 2 (figure 2).

FIGURE 2

4 Place and close a stainless steel jump ring (A) through both a new barrel bead and the barrel bead from step 2 (figure 3).

FIGURE 3

5 Place and close a bronze jump ring (B) through the same two barrel beads as the previous step, making sure that the bronze jump ring (B) is on the same side of the chain as the bronze jump ring (B) that was added in step 3 (figure 4).

FIGURE 4

6 Repeat steps 4 and 5 to continue your chain to the desired length.

Wallet Chain

Finished Size About 23 inches (58.4 cm)

MATERIALS

46 stainless steel jump rings, 18 gauge,
   5/16-inch ID (A)

46 bronze jump rings, 18 gauge, 5/16-inch ID (B)

45 barrel beads, 6 mm long with 5-mm hole

3/4-inch split ring

5/8-inch scissor snap

INSTRUCTIONS

1. Open all 46 stainless steel jump rings (A) and all 46 bronze jump rings (B).

2. Following the Chain Gang Variation Instructions, create a length of chain that consists of 45 stainless steel jump rings (A), paired with 45 bronze jump rings (B) and 45 barrel beads.

3. Slide a split ring through the final barrel bead from one end of the chain, as shown in figure 5.

FIGURE 5

4. Place and close an open stainless steel jump ring (A) through both the final two jump rings (one stainless steel, one bronze) from the other end of the chain and the loop of a scissor snap.

5. Repeat step 4 a total of three more times with the remaining stainless steel jump ring (A) and the two remaining bronze jump rings (B), making sure that the two bronze jump rings (B) sit between the two stainless jump rings (A), as shown in figure 6.

FIGURE 6

Boot Chain

Finished Size 13½ inches (34.3 cm)

MATERIALS

30 stainless steel jump rings, 18 gauge, ⁵/₁₆-inch ID (A)

30 bronze jump rings, 18 gauge, ⁵/₁₆-inch ID (B)

Stainless steel jump ring, 16 gauge, ⁵/₁₆-inch ID (C)

30 barrel beads, 6 mm long with 5-mm hole

Fold-over clasp, 4 x 13 mm

INSTRUCTIONS

1   Open all 30 stainless steel jump rings (A) and all 30 bronze jump rings (B).

2   Following the Chain Gang Variation Instructions on page 92 create a length of chain that consists of 30 stainless steel jump rings (A), paired with 30 bronze jump rings (B) and 30 barrel beads.

3   Place and close an open stainless steel jump ring (C) through both the final barrel bead from one end of the chain and the loop of a fold-over clasp. This clasp will attach to the final two jump rings (one stainless, one bronze) from the other end of the chain.

Key Chain

Finished Size 3½ inches (8.9 cm)

MATERIALS

6 stainless steel jump rings, 18 gauge, ⁵/₁₆-inch ID (A)

6 bronze jump rings, 18 gauge, ⁵/₁₆-inch ID (B)

7 barrel beads, 6 mm long with 5-mm hole

¾-inch split ring

INSTRUCTIONS

1   Open all six stainless steel jump rings (A) and all six bronze jump rings (B).

2   Following the Chain Gang Variation Instructions on page 92, create a length of chain that consists of six stainless steel jump rings (A), paired with six bronze jump rings (B) and seven barrel beads. This means that unlike the basic technique, both ends of this chain will end with a barrel bead.

3   Slide a split ring through the final barrel bead from one end of the chain.

Flower Mail Choker & Bracelet

Rows of cable chains connected in a hex pattern create the Japanese pattern known as *Hana-Gusari* or *Flower Mail*. The bracelet in this set includes cobalt blue beads and blue O-rings, creating an even more floral array.

Choker

Finished Size Approximately 16 inches (40.6 cm) in circumference

MATERIALS

154 stainless steel jump rings, 20 gauge, 1/8-inch ID (A)

16-gauge bronze jump rings, as follows:
- 59 with a 1/4-inch ID (B)
- 3 with a 7/32-inch ID (C)

73 cobalt glass roller beads, 6 mm

Stainless steel lobster clasp, 15 mm

INSTRUCTIONS

1 Open all 154 jump rings (A), 53 of the jump rings (B), and all three jump rings (C). Close the other six jump rings (B).

2 One at a time, place and close 34 open jump rings (B) through one roller bead each.

3 One at a time, place and close 18 open jump rings (B) through two roller beads each.

4 One at a time, place and close three open jump rings (C) through one roller bead each.

5 Place and close an open jump ring (B) through the loop of a clasp.

6 One at a time, place and close two open jump rings (A) through two of the closed jump rings (B) with roller beads prepared in step 2.

7 One at a time, place and close two open jump rings (A) through both one of the closed jump rings (B) with a roller bead prepared in step 6 and a new closed jump ring (B) with a roller bead attached. Note that all of the roller beads should sit to the same side of the chain (figure 1).

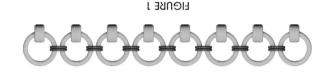

FIGURE 1

8 Repeat step 7 a total of 31 more times to create a chain that consists of the 34 closed jump rings (B) with roller beads attached.

9 One at a time, place and close two open jump rings (A) through both the chain's first closed jump ring (B) with a roller bead and a closed jump ring (B) with two roller beads created in step 3, making sure that the roller bead on the closed jump ring (B) sits to the left of jump rings (A) being added, as shown in figure 2.

FIGURE 2

10 One at a time, place and close two open jump rings (A) through both the second closed jump ring (B) with a roller bead from the chain and the closed jump ring (B) with two roller beads added in step 9, making sure that the roller bead from the closed jump ring (B) sits to the right of the closed jump ring (B) with two roller beads added, as shown in figure 3.

FIGURE 3

11 Repeat the process for adding closed jump rings (B) with two roller beads from steps 9 and 10 a total of 16 more times, each time using the next two closed jump rings (B) with roller beads from the chain as the attachment points.

12 Counting from left to right, locate the eighth closed jump ring (B) with two roller beads that was added to the chain in step 11. Between the two roller beads, one at a time, place and close two open jump rings (A) through both this jump ring and one of the closed jump rings (C) with a roller bead created in step 4.

13 Repeat step 12, except this time with the 10th closed jump ring (B) with two roller beads added to the chain during step 11.

14 Counting from left to right, locate the ninth closed jump ring (B) with two roller beads added to the chain during step 11. Between the two roller beads, one at a time, place and close two open jump rings (A) through both this jump ring (B) and the final closed jump ring (B) with two roller beads created in step 3.

Bracelet

Finished Size Approximately 7 inches (17.8 cm) in circumference

MATERIALS

168 stainless steel jump rings, 20 gauge, 1/8-inch ID (A)

36 bronze jump rings, 16 gauge, 1/4-inch ID (B)

11 blue neoprene O-rings, 16 gauge, 1/4-inch ID (C)

42 cobalt glass roller beads, 6 mm

INSTRUCTIONS

1 Open all 168 jump rings (A) and all 36 jump rings (B).

2 One at a time, place and close 30 open jump rings (B) through one roller bead each.

3 One at a time, place and close six open jump rings (B) through two roller beads each.

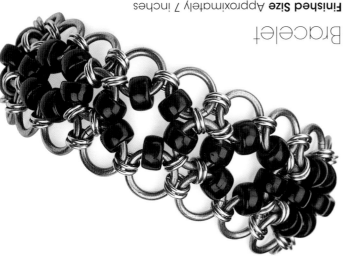

15 Between the two roller beads on the closed jump ring (B) added in step 14, one at a time, place and close two open jump rings (A) through this jump ring and the final closed jump rings (C) with a roller bead attached that was created in step 4.

16 One at a time, place and close two open jump rings (A) through both the final closed jump ring (B) with a roller bead from one end of the chain and the closed jump ring (B) with a roller bead prepared in step 5, making sure that the roller bead on the closed jump ring (B) stays to the bead side of the chain.

17 One at a time, place and close two open jump rings (A) through both the final closed jump ring (B) with a roller bead from the other end of the chain and a new closed jump ring (B), making sure that the roller bead on the final closed jump ring (B) from this end of the chain stays to the bead side of the chain.

18 One at a time, place and close two open jump rings (A) through both the closed jump ring (B) added in the previous step and a new closed jump ring (B).

19 Repeat step 18 a total of four more times to complete an adjustment chain consisting of a total of six closed jump rings (B).

4   Repeat steps 6 and 7 of the choker instructions to create a chain that consists of the 30 closed jump rings (B) with roller beads created in step 2.

5   One at a time, place and close two open jump rings (A) through the first and last closed jump rings (B) with roller beads from the chain created in step 4, making sure that all of the roller beads sit to the same side of the continuous chain.

6   Lay out the continuous chain as shown in figure 4.

FIGURE 4

7   One at a time, place and close eight open jump rings (A) through both the four closed jump rings (B) with roller beads and a new closed jump ring (B) with two roller beads, as shown in figure 5.

FIGURE 5

8   Repeat step 7 a total of five more times (figure 6). Set this section of chain aside.

FIGURE 6

9   One at a time, place and close two open jump rings (A) through two neoprene O-rings (C).

10 One at a time, place and close two open jump rings (A) through both one of the neoprene O-rings (C) from step 9 and a new neoprene O-ring (C).

11 Repeat step 10 once to create a length of chain consisting of four neoprene O-rings (C).

12 Repeat steps 9, 10, and 11 to create a second length of chain consisting of four neoprene O-rings (C).

13 Repeat steps 9 and 10 to create a third length of chain consisting of three neoprene O-rings (C).

14 Lay out the three lengths of chain completed in steps 9 through 13 as shown in figure 7.

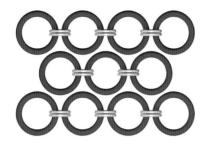

FIGURE 7

15 One at a time, place and close 24 open jump rings (A) through the three neoprene O-ring (C) chains in pairs, as shown in figure 8, to create a small piece of Hana-Gusari chain.

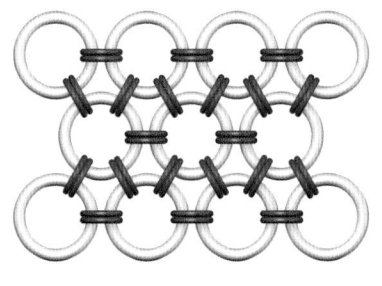

FIGURE 8

16 Place the piece of neoprene Hana-Gusari chain between the ends of the bronze and bead chain set aside in step 8, as shown in figure 9.

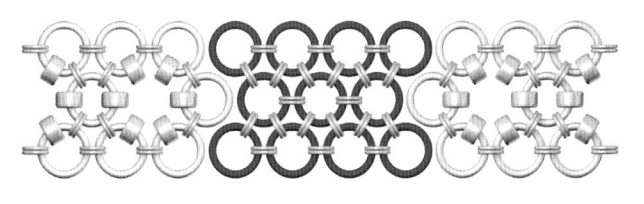

FIGURE 9

17 One at a time, place and close 20 open jump rings (A) through the neoprene O-rings and closed jump rings (B) in pairs, as shown in figure 10, to complete the bracelet as a continuous loop.

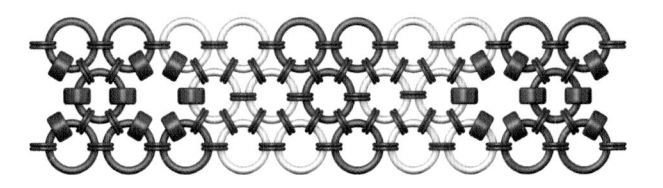

FIGURE 10

Cable Cross
Bracelet & Earrings

Topaz beads make this subtle and sunny bi-metal bracelet and earring set a perfect gift for a November birthday.

Bracelet

Finished Size Approximately 8 inches (20.3 cm) in circumference

MATERIALS

138 sterling silver jump rings, 21 gauge, 3/32-inch ID (A)

7 gold-filled jump rings, 16 gauge, 9/32-inch ID (B)

12 gold-filled jump rings, 18 gauge, 5/32-inch ID (C)

1 sterling silver jump ring, 18 gauge, 1/8-inch ID (D)

14 topaz glass roller beads, 6 mm (E)

16 silver-lined topaz glass "E" beads, size 6/0 (F)

Gold-filled lobster claw clasp, 11.7 mm

INSTRUCTIONS

1 Open 80 of the jump rings (A), all seven jump rings (B), eight of the jump rings (C), and the one jump ring (D). Close the other 58 jump rings (A) and the four remaining jump rings (C).

2 Following the basic directions for creating Double Cable chain on page 24, create seven lengths of Double Cable chain that consist of a total of seven jump ring (A) pairs each.

3 Place and close an open jump ring (B) through both the second and sixth jump ring pair from a Double Cable chain created in step 2 and two roller beads (E), as shown in figure 1.

FIGURE 1

4 Repeat step 3 with the remaining six Double Cable chains created in step 2 to create a total of seven Double Cable sections.

5 One at a time, place a total of eight open jump rings (C) through two beads (F) each. Close the jump rings.

6 One at a time, place and close two open jump rings (A) through both the pair of closed jump rings (A) from one end of a Double Cable section completed in step 4 and one of the closed jump rings (C) with two beads created in step 5.

7 One at a time, place and close two open jump rings (A) through both the pair of closed jump rings (A) from the other end of the Double Cable section added to in step 6 and one of the closed jump rings (C) with beads (F) created in step 5.

8 One at a time, place and close two open jump rings (A) through both the pair of closed jump rings (A) from the end of a new Double Cable section completed in step 4 and the closed jump rings (C) with two beads added in step 7. Make sure that the jump rings added sit between the two beads on the closed jump ring (C) and that the jump ring (B) on the Double Cable section being added is on the same side of the chain as the original Double Cable section from step 6, as shown in figure 2.

FIGURE 2

9 Repeat steps 7 and 8 a total of five more times, adding the closed jump rings (C) with two beads (F) created in step 4 and the Double Cable sections completed in step 4, in turn.

10 Repeat step 7 one more time, ending the chain with a closed jump ring (C) with two beads (F) attached.

11 One at a time, place and close two open jump rings (A) through both the closed jump rings (C) with two beads (F) added in step 10 and a closed jump ring (C), making sure that the jump rings added sit between the two beads (F) on the closed jump ring (C).

12 One at a time, place and close two open jump rings (A) through both the closed jump ring (C) added in step 11 and a new closed jump ring (C).

13 Repeat step 12 twice more to finish the adjustment chain on this end of the bracelet.

14 On the opposite end of the chain, one at a time, place and close two open jump rings (A) through two closed jump rings (A).

15 Finish the bracelet by placing and closing the open jump ring (D) through both the two closed jump rings (A) added in step 14 and the loop of a clasp.

Earrings

Finished Size Approximately 1½ inches (3.8 cm) long

MATERIALS

48 sterling silver jump rings, 21 gauge,
  ³/₃₂-inch ID (A)

2 gold-filled jump rings, 16 gauge, ⁹/₃₂-inch ID (B)

2 gold-filled jump rings, 18 gauge, ⁵/₃₂-inch ID (C)

2 topaz glass roller beads, 6 mm (D)

2 silver-lined topaz glass "E" beads, size 6/0 (E)

2 stainless steel French hooks

INSTRUCTIONS

1　Open 24 of the jump rings (A), both jump rings (B), and both jump rings (C). Close the other 24 jump rings (A).

2　Following the basic directions for creating Double Cable Chain on page 24, create a length of Double Cable chain that consists of a total of nine jump ring (A) pairs.

3　Place and close an open jump ring (B) through both the second and sixth jump ring pair from a Double Cable chain created in step 2 and two roller beads (D), in the same manner as step 3 of the bracelet instructions.

4　Place and close an open jump ring (C) through two beads (E).

5　One at a time, place and close two open jump rings (A) through both the pair of closed jump rings (A) from the short end of the Double Cable section completed in step 3 and the closed jump ring (C) with two beads (E) created in step 4, shown in figure 3.

FIGURE 3

6　One at a time, place and close two open jump rings (A) through the closed jump rings (C) with two beads (E), added in step 5, making sure that the jump rings being added sit between the two beads (E) on the closed jump ring (C).

7　One at a time, place and close two open jump rings (A) through both the two closed jump rings (C) added in step 6 and the loop of a French hook.

8　Repeat steps 2 through 7 to create a second identical earring.

Red Carpet
Cable Set

To make this three-piece set, you employ a technique to create an offset cable that is basically a bias-cut slice of European chain with a finely beaded edge.

OFFSET CABLE TECHNIQUE INSTRUCTIONS

1 Open all the jump rings required for the project, except where you are specifically instructed to close rings for adjustment chains, etc.

2 Place and close one-quarter of the jump rings required for the project through beads appropriate to the dimensions of the jump rings (figure 1). See page 15 for specific size information.

FIGURE 1

3 Place and close an open jump ring through two of the jump rings with beads prepared in step 2 and through a new bead (figure 2).

FIGURE 2

4 Place and close an open jump ring through one of the end jump rings with beads from step 3, a new jump ring with bead that was prepared in step 1, and a new bead (figure 3).

FIGURE 3

5 Newly added beads must sit to the same side of the cable chain as each other. The beads added on jump rings prepared in step 2 must sit to the same side of the cable chain as each other (figure 3). Make sure neither spirals around the cable chain as in figure 4, which shows a bead that has mistakenly slipped.

FIGURE 4

6 Repeat the process of step 4, placing and closing open jump rings through the end jump rings with beads of the main cable chain, new jump rings with beads, and new beads until all of the jump rings with beads prepared in step 2 have been used to create the main cable chain (figure 5).

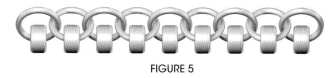

FIGURE 5

7 Returning to the start of the main cable chain, place and close an open jump ring through the end jump ring with a bead from the main cable chain and then a new bead (figure 6).

FIGURE 6

8 Place and close an open jump ring through the jump ring with a bead added in step 7, the jump ring from the main cable chain as indicated in the illustration, and a new bead. The correct placement of the added bead is on the edge of the chain, as in figure 7.

FIGURE 7

9 Place and close an open jump ring through the jump ring with bead added in step 8, the jump ring from the main cable chain as indicated in the illustration, and a new bead. The correct placement of the added bead is on the edge of the chain, as in figure 8.

FIGURE 8

10 Continue the process of adding new jump rings and beads as in steps 8 and 9 until the entire length of the main cable chain has been doubled into an offset cable chain.

Bracelet

Finished Size Approximately 8½ inches (21.6 cm) in circumference

MATERIALS

72 sterling silver jump rings, 16 gauge, 7/32-inch ID (A)

8 sterling silver jump rings, 18 gauge, 1/8-inch ID (B)

67 silver-lined crystal, square-holed glass beads, size 2/0

1 sterling silver lobster claw clasp, 8 x 4 mm

INSTRUCTIONS

1 Open the 72 jump rings (A), and close the eight jump rings (B).

2 Prepare 17 jump rings (A) by placing and closing each one through a bead.

3 Using the prepared jump rings (A) with beads from step 2, follow steps 3 through 5 of the Offset Cable Technique Instructions on page 107 to create a main cable chain that is 33 closed jump rings with beads in length.

4 Follow steps 6 through 10 of the basic Offset Cable technique to create an offset cable chain that is a total of 66 closed jump rings (A) with beads in length.

5 Place and close an open jump ring (A) through both closed jump rings (A) from one end of the offset cable chain and the loop of a clasp (figure 9).

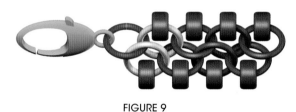

FIGURE 9

6 Place and close an open jump ring (A) through both closed jump rings (A) from the other end of the offset cable chain and two closed jump rings (B) (figure 10).

FIGURE 10

7 Create a short adjustment chain by placing and closing an open jump ring (A) through both the two closed jump rings (B) added in the previous step and two new closed jump rings (B) a total of three times.

8 Finish the short adjustment chain and bracelet by placing and closing an open jump ring (A) through the final two closed jump rings (B) added in the previous step and through a single bead (figure 11).

FIGURE 11

Choker

Finished Size Approximately 14 inches (35.6 cm) in circumference

MATERIALS

164 sterling silver jump rings, 18 gauge, $^5/_{32}$-inch ID (A)

8 spring hard sterling silver jump rings, 21 gauge, $^3/_{32}$-inch ID (B)

158 silver-lined crystal, square-hole glass beads, size 6/0

1 sterling silver lobster claw clasp, 8 x 4 mm

INSTRUCTIONS

1 Open all 164 jump rings (A), and close the eight jump rings (B).

2 Prepare 40 jump rings (A) by placing and closing each one through a bead.

3   Using the prepared jump rings (A) with beads from step 2, follow steps 3 through 5 of the Offset Cable Technique Instructions on page 107 to create a main cable chain that is 79 closed jump rings (A) with beads in length.

4   Follow steps 6 through 10 of the basic Offset Cable technique to create an offset cable chain that is a total of 158 closed jump rings (A) with beads in length.

5   Place and close an open jump ring (A) through two closed jump rings (A) from one end of the Offset Cable chain and the loop of a clasp (figure 9).

6   Place and close an open jump ring (A) through two closed jump rings (A) from the other end of the Offset Cable chain and two closed jump rings (B). See figure 10.

7   Create a short adjustment chain by placing and closing an open jump ring (A) through both the two closed jump rings (B) added in the previous step and two new closed jump rings (B) a total of three times.

8   Finish the short adjustment chain and choker by placing and closing an open jump ring (A) through both the final two closed jump rings (B) added in the previous step and a single bead (figure 11).

Earrings

Finished Size Approximately 1½ inches (3.8 cm) long

MATERIALS

21-gauge spring hard sterling silver jump rings, as follows:

- 46 with a ⅛-inch ID (A)
- 2 with a ³⁄₃₂-inch ID (B)

46 silver-lined crystal, square-hole glass beads, size 8/0

2 surgical stainless steel 4-mm ball posts with loops and butterfly nuts

1   Open the 46 jump rings (A) and the two jump rings (B).

2   Prepare six jump rings (A) by placing and closing each one through a bead.

3 Using the prepared jump rings (A) with beads from step 2, follow steps 3 through 5 of the Offset Cable Technique Instructions on page 107 to create a main cable chain that is 11 closed jump rings (A) with beads in length.

4 Follow steps 6 through 10 of the basic Offset Cable technique to create an offset cable chain that is a total of 22 closed jump rings (A) with beads in length.

5 Place and close an open jump ring (A) through two closed jump rings (A) from one end of the offset cable chain and a new bead (figure 12).

FIGURE 12

6 Finish the earring by placing and closing an open jump ring (B) through both two closed jump rings (A) from the other end of the offset cable chain and the loop of a ball post (figure 13).

FIGURE 13

7 To create the second earring as a mirror image of the first, follow steps 2 through 6, except that during step 5, place and close the open jump ring (A) through the opposite end of the offset cable chain before adding the new bead.

Grape Leaf Earrings

Fine earrings with a simple design, these inverted triangles are reminiscent of grape leaves in autumn.

Finished Size Approximately 1¼ inches (3.2 cm) long

MATERIALS

2 sterling silver jump rings, 16 gauge, ⁹/₃₂-inch ID (A)

92 spring hard sterling silver jump rings, 21 gauge, ³/₃₂-inch ID (B)

34 garnet glass seed beads, size 11/0

2 surgical stainless steel 4-mm ball posts with loops and butterfly nuts

INSTRUCTIONS

1 Open both large jump rings (A) and 78 of the small jump rings (B). Close the remaining 14 small jump rings (B).

2 One at a time, place and close two small jump rings (B) through one seed bead each.

3 Place and close a large jump ring (A) through the two small jump rings (B) with seed beads prepared in step 2 and seven closed small jump rings (B). You should add these small jump rings in this order: one small jump ring (B) with a seed bead attached, seven closed small jump rings (B), and then the other small jump ring (B) with a seed bead, as shown in figure 1.

FIGURE 1

4 Following the instructions for the basic European 1 in 4 pattern on page 28 (with the exception of adding a single new row at a time by not adding any closed rings during steps 5 and 6 of the basic European 1 in 4 pattern), use the nine small closed jump rings (B) added in step 3, two new seed beads, and eight new open small jump rings (B) as the base to create a new row consisting of eight small jump rings (B). Each row begins and ends with a small jump ring (B) with a seed bead, as shown in figure 2.

FIGURE 2

5 Repeat the previous step a total of six more times, adding a total of six more rows to the earring, with each row consisting of one fewer small jump ring (B) each time the step is repeated. Always begin and end by closing the small jump ring (B) through a new seed bead as well as through the two small jump rings (B) from the main pattern.

6 Place and close a final small open jump ring (B) through both the two small jump rings (B) with seed beads added during the final part of step 5 and a new seed bead.

7 Finish the earring by placing and closing a small open jump ring (B) through both the large jump rings (A) and the loop of a ball post.

8 To create the second earring, follow steps 2 through 7, except that base rows of small closed jump rings (B) attached in step 3 should overlap in the opposite direction of the base rows of the first earring (figure 3).

FIGURE 3

Bronze Age Bolo Tie

Here's a bronze chain tie that's just the thing for any man who's looking for something different, yet classy.

Finished Size Approximately 40 inches (101.6 cm) in length

Wrapped Donut

MATERIALS

20-gauge stainless steel jump rings, as follows:

- 126 with a $7/64$-inch ID (A)
- 30 with a $5/32$-inch ID (B)

30 bronze jump rings, 18 gauge, $5/32$-inch ID (C)

2 bronze jump rings, 16 gauge, $5/16$-inch ID (D)

1 "tiger iron" gemstone donut, 40 mm

INSTRUCTIONS

1. Open all 126 jump rings (A) and the two jump rings (D). Close all 30 jump rings (B) and all 30 jump rings (C).

2. One at a time, place and close two open jump rings (A) through two closed jump rings (C).

3. One at a time, place and close two open jump rings (A) through both one of the closed jump rings (C) from step 2 and a new closed jump ring (C).

4. Repeat step 3 a total of 12 more times to create a length of cable chain that is 15 jump rings (C) in length, held together by 14 jump ring (A) pairs.

5. Repeat steps 2 through 4 to create a second identical length of cable chain.

6. One at a time, place and close two open jump rings (A) through both the first closed jump ring (C) from the end of one of the Double Cable chains and two closed jump rings (B).

7. One at a time, place and close two open jump rings (A) through both the two closed jump rings (B) from step 6 and the first closed jump ring (C) from the end of the other Double Cable chain, as shown in figure 1.

FIGURE 1

117

8 Repeat steps 6 and 7 a total of 14 more times, connecting the two Double Cable chains as shown in figure 2.

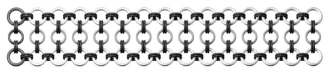

FIGURE 2

9 One at a time, place and close two open jump rings (A) through the first and 15th closed jump rings (C) of one of the Double Cable chains.

10 Fold the Double Cable chains over the gemstone donut so that the closed Double Cable chain completed in step 9 sits on one face of the gemstone donut, the other open Double Cable chain sits on the opposite face of the gemstone donut, and the 15 pairs of closed jump rings (B) sit on the edge of the gemstone donut.

11 One at a time, place and close two open jump rings (A) through the first and 15th closed jump rings (C) of the open Double Cable chain to lock all of the chains in place around the gemstone donut. Note that sometimes imperfections in the size of gemstone donuts may make it impossible to use jump rings (A) to lock all of the chain in place. If this happens, simply substitute slightly larger jump rings and make sure this face of the gemstone donut sits to the back of necklace, so the jump ring size disparity is unnoticeable.

12 One at a time, place and close two open jump rings (A) through a pair of closed jump rings (A) on the back face of the wrapped gemstone donut.

13 One at a time, place and close two open jump rings (A) through the next pair of closed jump rings (A) on the back face of the wrapped gemstone donut.

14 One at a time, place and close two open jump rings (A) through the next pair of closed jump rings (A) on the back face of the wrapped gemstone donut.

15 Place and close an open jump ring (D) through both the two jump rings (A) added in step 12 and one of the jump rings (A) added in step 13.

16 Place and close an open jump ring (D) through the other jump ring (A) added in step 13, the two jump rings (A) added in step 14, and the jump ring (D) added in step 15, as shown in figure 3.

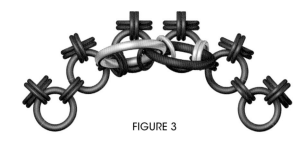

FIGURE 3

Bolo Tie Chain

MATERIALS

18-gauge bronze jump rings, as follows:

- ○ 250 with a $\frac{3}{16}$-inch ID (A)
- ○ 500 with a $\frac{5}{32}$-inch ID (B)
- ○ 4 with a $\frac{1}{4}$-inch ID (C)

INSTRUCTIONS

1 Open all 250 jump rings (A), 250 of the jump rings (B), and two of the jump rings (C). Close the other 250 jump rings (B) and the other two jump rings (C).

2 Following the instructions for Byzantine chain on page 30, construct a length of Byzantine chain that consists of a total of 250 jump rings (A) and 500 jump rings (B).

3 Place a closed jump ring (C) between the two closed jump rings (A) from one end of the chain, as shown in figure 4.

FIGURE 4

4 Place and close an open jump ring (C) through both the two jump rings (A) from the same end of the chain as step 3 and the closed jump ring (C) from step 3, as shown in figure 5.

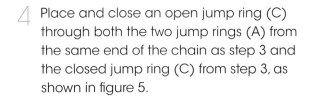

FIGURE 5

5 Feed the other end of the Byzantine chain completed in step 2 up through the closed jump ring (D) added to the back of the wrapped gemstone donut in step 15 and back down through the other closed jump ring (D) added to the back of the wrapped gemstone donut in step 16.

6 Repeat steps 3 and 4 on the other end of the Byzantine chain completed in step 2 to prevent the wrapped gemstone donut from slipping off the Byzantine chain.

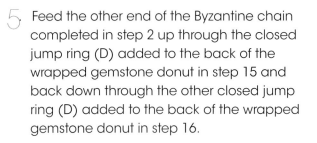

Zipper Charms

These saucy little pieces, shown here in four patterns, are perfect for dressing up anything from jackets to purses. In winter, they make it easy to pull up zippers while wearing mittens.

Double Cable Zipper Pull

Finished Size Approximately 2½ inches (6.4 cm) long without the hook

MATERIALS

18-gauge stainless steel jump rings, as follows:

- 2 with a ⁵⁄₁₆-inch ID (A)
- 2 with a ¼-inch ID (B)
- 2 with a ⁷⁄₃₂-inch ID (C)
- 4 with a ³⁄₁₆-inch ID (D)
- 10 with a ⁵⁄₃₂-inch ID (E)

Black triangular glass hair pendant bead (also known as *Talhakimt* or *Taunfaulk* beads), 18 mm

Spring steel lanyard hook, 20–23 x 6 mm

INSTRUCTIONS

1   Open two jump rings (D) and eight of the jump rings (E). Close both jump rings (A), both jump rings (B), both jump rings (C), the last two jump rings (D), and the last two jump rings (E).

2   Following the basic instructions for creating a Double Cable pattern chain on page 24, create a length of Double Cable chain that consists of five pairs of jump rings (A, B, C, D, and E), connected together in order of descending size by four pairs of jump rings (E) as shown in figure 1.

FIGURE 1

3   One at a time, place and close two open jump rings (D) through both the two closed jump rings (E) from one end of the Double Cable chain and the triangular bead.

4   Complete the zipper pull by attaching the lanyard hook through the two closed jump rings (A) from the opposite end of the Double Cable chain (figure 2).

FIGURE 2

Persian Star Zipper Pull

Finished Size Approximately 1½ inches (3.8 cm) long without the hook

MATERIALS

18-gauge stainless steel jump rings, as follows:

2 with a ⁵⁄₁₆-inch ID (A)

5 with a ¼-inch ID (B)

2 with a ³⁄₁₆-inch ID (C)

5 with a ⁵⁄₃₂-inch ID (D)

Capri glass crow bead, 9 x 6 mm

Spring steel lanyard hook, 20–23 x 6 mm

INSTRUCTIONS

1 Open all the jump rings (A to D) you'll need to complete this project.

2 Following the basic instructions for creating a Persian Star pattern chain on page 36, create a length of Persian Star chain that consists of five jump rings (B) and five jump rings (D), as shown in figure 3.

FIGURE 3

3 Place and close an open jump ring (A) through both the closed jump ring (D) from one end of the Persian Star chain and a crow bead (figure 4).

FIGURE 4

4 Repeat the previous step, placing and closing a second open jump ring (A) through the same closed jump ring (D) from one end of the Persian Star chain and the same crow bead. However, add this ring on the opposite side of the closed jump ring (B) from the same end of the Persian Star chain, pinning the jump ring (B) between the jump rings (A) added in this step and in the previous step, as shown in figure 5.

FIGURE 5

5 Place and close an open jump ring (C) through the closed jump ring (D) from the opposite end of the Persian Star chain and the lanyard hook (figure 6).

FIGURE 6

6   Complete the zipper pull by repeating the previous step, placing and closing a second open jump ring (C) through the same closed jump ring (D) from one end of the Persian Star chain and the same lanyard hook. However, add this ring on the opposite side of the closed jump ring (B) from the same end of the Persian Star chain, pinning the jump ring (B) between the jump rings (D) added in this step and in the previous step, as shown in figure 7.

FIGURE 7

Double Spiral Zipper Pull

Finished Size Approximately 1½ inches (3.8 cm) long without the hook

MATERIALS

18-gauge stainless steel jump rings, as follows:

○   1 with a ⁵⁄₁₆-inch ID (A)

○   20 with a ⁷⁄₃₂-inch ID (B)

3 green lustre glass roller beads, 6 x 4 mm

Spring steel lanyard hook, 20–23 x 6 mm

INSTRUCTIONS

1   Open the one jump ring (A) and 18 of the jump rings (B). Close the last two jump rings (B).

2   Following the basic instructions for creating a Double Spiral pattern chain on page 26, create a length of Double Spiral chain that consists of 20 closed jump rings (B) in 10 pairs, as shown in figure 8.

FIGURE 8

3   Following the twist of the Double Spiral chain, place and close an open jump ring (A) through the four closed jump rings (B) from one end of the Double Spiral chain and three roller beads.

4   Complete the zipper pull by attaching the lanyard hook through the four closed jump rings (B) from the opposite end of the Double Spiral chain, following the twist of the Double Spiral chain (figure 9).

FIGURE 9

Rings of Saturn
Zipper Pull

Finished Size Approximately 1¾ inches (4.4 cm) long without the hook

MATERIALS

18-gauge stainless steel jump rings, as follows:

- 4 with a ⁵⁄₁₆-inch ID (A)
- 16 with a ³⁄₁₆-inch ID (B)

2 red lustre glass crow beads, 9 mm

Spring steel lanyard hook, 20–23 x 6 mm

INSTRUCTIONS

1 Open three of the jump rings (A) and nine of the jump rings (B). Close the last jump ring (A) and seven other jump rings (B).

2 Following the basic instructions for creating a Rings of Saturn pattern chain on page 33, create a length of Rings of Saturn chain that consists of three jump rings (A) and 16 jump rings (B), as shown in figure 10. Note that this Rings of Saturn pattern chain is missing a jump ring (B) that would normally complete one end of the chain.

FIGURE 10

3 Place and close an open jump ring (A) through the two closed jump rings (B) from the end of the Rings of Saturn chain noted in step 2 and two crow beads (figure 11). Note that this replaces the missing jump ring (B) from the end of the chain.

FIGURE 11

4 Complete the zipper pull by attaching the lanyard hook through the closed jump ring (A) and the closed jump ring (B) from the opposite end of the Rings of Saturn chain (figure 12).

FIGURE 12

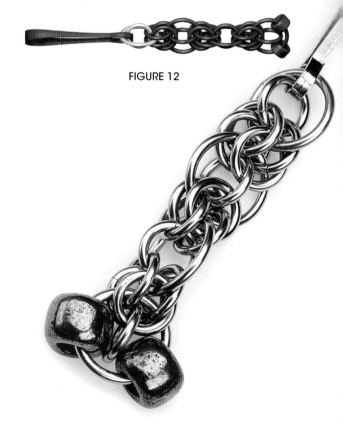

Andromeda Necklace

This attention-grabbing, multi-tiered neck-lace is a perfect showcase for the most spectacular focal beads you can find.

Finished Size Approximately 16 inches (40.6 cm) circumference around the neck

MATERIALS

18-gauge sterling silver jump rings, as follows:

- ○ 348 with a ⁵/₃₂-inch ID (A)
- ○ 54 with a ³/₁₆-inch ID (B)
- ○ 76 with a ⁷/₃₂-inch ID (C)
- ○ 88 with a ¹/₄-inch ID (D)
- ○ 6 with a ⁵/₁₆-inch ID (E)

20-gauge sterling silver jump rings, as follows:

- ○ 44 (approximately) with a ³/₃₂-inch ID (F)
- ○ 8 with a ⁷/₆₄-inch ID (G)

2 to 4 large focal beads, minimum hole size 4.5 mm, 1 to 1¹/₂ inch (2.5 to 3.8 cm) in length

Sterling silver infinity clasp, 13 x 7 mm

INSTRUCTIONS

1 Open 290 of the jump rings (A), two of the jump rings (B), six of the jump rings (D), 20 of the jump rings (F), and six of the jump rings (G). Close the other 58 jump rings (A), the last 52 jump rings (B), all 76 jump rings (C), the remaining 82 jump rings (D), all six jump rings (E), the other 24 jump rings (F), and the last two jump rings (G).

DESIGN TIP
Always remember that lampworking and chain making go hand in hand! A lamp-working friend of mine, who wishes to remain anonymous, created these Galaxy Swirl Beads especially for me. Don't be afraid to commission specialty focal beads of your own or track down focal bead substitutions; just make sure that your focal beads have at least a 4.5-mm hole. If they don't, you will have to use a bead reamer to enlarge the hole to a point where you can fit a chain through

2 Following the directions on page 24, create the following Double Cable chains:

- ○ Two Double Cable chains consisting of 18 pairs of jump rings (D), connected by 17 pairs of jump rings (A). Mark these Double Cable chains as (Z).

- ○ Two Double Cable chains consisting of 15 pairs of jump rings (C), connected by 14 pairs of jump rings (A). Mark these Double Cable chains as (Y).

- ○ Two Double Cable chains consisting of 10 pairs of jump rings (B) and ending with a pair of jump rings (C), connected by of 10 pairs of jump rings (A). Mark these Double Cable chains as (X).

○ One Double Cable chain of the following pattern of jump ring pairs, connected by a total of 47 pairs of jump rings (A):

- Jump ring pair (E)
- Jump ring pair (D)
- Jump ring pair (C)
- Jump ring pair (B)
- Seven jump ring pairs (A)
- Jump ring pair (B)
- Jump ring pair (C)
- Jump ring pair (D)
- Jump ring pair (E)
- Jump ring pair (D)
- Jump ring pair (C)
- Jump ring pair (B)
- 15 jump ring pairs (A)
- Jump ring pair (B)
- Jump ring pair (C)
- Jump ring pair (D)
- Jump ring pair (E)
- Jump ring pair (D)
- Jump ring pair (C)
- Jump ring pair (B)
- Seven jump ring pairs (A)
- Jump ring pair (B) through the loop of a clasp

○ Mark this Double Cable chain as (W) and place temporary ring markers on the following jump ring pairs: 15th (E), 16th (D), 17th (C), 27th (A), 36th (D), 37th (E), and 38th (D).

○ One Double Cable chain consisting of a pair of jump rings (B), connected to a pair of jump rings (C) by a pair of jump rings (A). Mark this Double Cable chain (V).

○ Two Double Cable chains consisting of pairs of jump rings (F). These Double Cable chains should be just long enough to reach through the vertical length of the holes in the large focal beads, as in Figure 1, or two large focal beads stacked together. It needs approximately 11 jump ring (F) pairs. Mark these Double Cable chains (U).

DESIGN TIP

If you simply cannot locate focal beads with large enough holes to fit these Double Cable chains through, it is perfectly acceptable to replace the Double Cable chains (U) with lengths of finer chain or even, as a last resort, a length of wire with wrapped loops at each end.

3 One at a time, place and close two open jump rings (G) through the pair of closed jump rings (F) from the end of one of the Double Cable chains (U).

4 One at a time, place and close two open jump rings (D) through the pair of jump rings (G) added in step 3.

5 Feed the Double Cable chain (U) from steps 3 and 4 through the hole of one or two large focal beads. Note that you may have to add or remove jump ring (F) pairs to make sure that the Double Cable chain (U) is the correct length to reach through the large focal bead.

6 One at a time, place and close two open jump rings (G) through the pair of jump rings (F) from the Double Cable chain (U) fed through the large focal bead in step 5. Note that the jump rings (G) added during this step should be as close to the large focal bead as possible.

DESIGN TIP

If you have trouble feeding the Double Cable chain (U) through the large focal bead, it may be helpful to tie a string or thread to the end of the Double Cable chain (U) to feed through the large focal bead first (figure 1).

FIGURE 1

7 One at a time, place and close two open jump rings (D) through the pair of jump rings (G) added in step 6. Note that this will lock the Double Cable chain (U) in place inside the large focal bead.

8 One at a time, place and close two open jump rings (G) through both the pair of jump rings (D) added in step 7 and the pair of jump rings (F) from one end of the second Double Cable chain (U).

9 Repeat steps 5 through 7, feeding the second Double Cable chain (U) through one or two new large focal beads and locking it in place.

10 One at a time, place and close two open jump rings (A) through both the 27th jump ring pair (A) of the Double Cable chain (W) and the closed jump ring (B) pair from the Double Cable chain (V).

11 One at a time, place and close two open jump rings (A) through both the closed jump ring (C) pair from the Double Cable chain (V) and the top closed jump ring (D) pair from one end of the cable and bead combination created in steps 5 through 9.

12 One at a time, place and close two open jump rings (A) through both the closed jump ring (B) pair from one end of the Double Cable chains (X) and the 17th jump ring (C) pair from the Double Cable chain (W).

13 One at a time, place and close two open jump rings (A) through both the closed jump ring (C) pair from the other end of the Double Cable chain (X) from step 12 and the left side of the top closed jump ring (D) pair attached in step 11.

14 Repeat steps 12 and 13 with the second Double Cable chain (X), the 36th jump ring (D) pair from the Double Cable chain (W), and the right side of the top closed jump ring (D) pair attached to in step 11.

15 One at a time, place and close two open jump rings (A) through both the closed jump ring (C) pair from one end of the Double Cable chains (Y) and the 18th jump ring (B) pair from the Double Cable chain (W).

16 One at a time, place and close two open jump rings (A) through both the closed jump ring (C) pair from the other end of the Double Cable chain (Y) from step 15 and the left side of the middle jump ring pair (D) added to the cable and bead combination in step 7.

17 Repeat steps 15 and 16 with the second Double Cable chain (Y), the 37th jump ring (E) pair from the Double Cable chain (W), and the right side of the middle jump ring pair (D) added to the cable and bead combination in step 7.

18 One at a time, place and close two open jump rings (A) through the closed jump ring (D) pair from one end of the Double Cable chains (Z) and the 19th jump ring (A) pair from the Double Cable chain (W).

19 One at a time, place and close two open jump rings (A) through both the closed jump ring (D) pair from the other end of the Double Cable chain (Z) from step 18 and the left side of the bottom jump ring pair (D) added to the cable and bead combination in step 4.

20 Repeat steps 18 and 19 with the second Double Cable chain (Z), the 38th jump ring (D) pair from the Double Cable chain (W), and the right side of the bottom jump ring pair (D) added to the cable and bead combination in step 4.

Orbital Earring Collection

This easy adaptation of the Single Cable chain pattern gives you a myriad of options for creating cool beaded earrings. This set highlights three different alternatives.

ORBITAL CABLE TECHNIQUE INSTRUCTIONS

Note that you will need jump rings to create this chain with a large enough inner diameter so that when you place two closed rings together, as illustrated in step 2, you can see enough of the vertical jump ring to place a new open jump link through.

1 Close three jump rings, and open two jump rings.

2 Place two closed jump rings together as illustrated, with one of the jump rings vertical and one horizontal (figure 1).

FIGURE 1

3 Place and close an open jump ring through the closed vertical jump ring from step 2, as shown in figure 2, pinning the horizontal closed jump ring between the closed vertical jump ring and the jump ring you are adding during this step.

FIGURE 2

4 Place a closed jump ring horizontally against the jump ring that you added in step 3, as illustrated in figure 3.

FIGURE 3

5 Place and close a new open jump ring through the jump ring added in step 3, as shown in figure 4, pinning the horizontal closed jump ring from step 4 between the jump ring added in step 3 and the jump ring you are adding during this step. Note that the ring ratio to continue this pattern is one open jump ring to one closed jump ring.

FIGURE 4

6 Repeat steps 4 and 5 to continue the pattern to the desired length.

Zircon Nebula Earrings

Finished Size About 1¼ inch (3.2 cm)

MATERIALS

14 sterling silver jump rings, 16 gauge,
⁹⁄₃₂-inch ID (A)

12 blue zircon glass roller beads, 6 mm (B)

14 teal translucent glass roller beads,
6 mm (C)

2 surgical stainless steel French hooks

INSTRUCTIONS

1   Open all 14 jump rings (A).

2   One at a time, place and close three jump
rings (A) through two roller beads (B) each.

3   Place and close a jump ring (A) through
three roller beads (C).

4   Place a closed jump
ring (A) with two roller
beads (B) created
in step 2 horizontally
against the closed
jump ring (A) with three
roller beads (C), as
shown in figure 5.

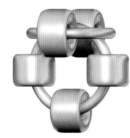

FIGURE 5

5   Place and close an
open jump ring (A)
through both the closed
jump ring (A) with three
roller beads (C) created
in step 3 and two new
roller beads (C), pinning
the closed jump ring (A)
with two roller beads (B)
from step 4 in place with
one roller bead (B) to
each side, as shown in figure 6.

FIGURE 6

6   Place a closed jump ring
(A) with two roller beads
(b) created in step 2 horizontally against the closed
jump ring (A) with two
roller beads (C) added in
step 5, with one roller bead
(C) to each side, as shown
in figure 7.

FIGURE 7

7 Place and close an open jump ring (A) through both the closed jump ring (A) with two roller beads (C) added in step 5 and two new roller beads (C), pinning the closed jump ring (A) with two roller beads (B) from step 6 in place with one roller bead (B) to each side, as shown in figure 8.

FIGURE 8

8 Place a closed jump ring (A) with two roller beads (B) created in step 2 horizontally against the closed jump ring (A) with two roller beads (C) added in step 7, with one roller bead (C) to each side, as shown in figure 9.

FIGURE 9

9 Place and close an open jump ring (A) through both the closed jump ring (A) with two roller beads (C) added in step 7 and the loop of a French hook, pinning the closed jump ring (A) with two roller beads (B) from step 8 in place with one roller bead (B) to each side, as shown in figure 10.

FIGURE 10

10 Repeat steps 2 through 9 exactly to create a second matched earring.

Orbital Sunrise Earrings

Finished Size ¾ inch (1.9 cm)

MATERIALS

10 sterling silver jump rings, 18 gauge, 15/64-inch ID (A)

10 frosted red glass beads, size 6/0 (B)

2 surgical stainless steel French hooks (C)

INSTRUCTIONS

1 Open six of the jump rings (A), and close the other four jump rings (A).

2 Place and close an open jump ring (A) through five glass beads (B).

3 Place a closed jump ring (A) horizontally against the jump ring (A) with five glass beads (B) created in step 2.

4 Place and close an open jump ring (A) through the jump ring (A) with five glass beads (B) created in step 2, pinning the horizontal closed jump ring (A) from step 3 in place as shown in figure 11.

FIGURE 11

133

5 Place a closed jump ring (A) horizontally against the jump ring added in step 4.

6 Place and close an open jump ring (A) through both the jump ring added in step 4 and the loop of a French hook (C), pinning the horizontal closed jump ring (A) from step 5 in place, as shown in figure 12.

FIGURE 12

7 Repeat steps 2 through 6 exactly to create a second matched earring.

Stardust Earrings

Finished Size 1¼ inch (3.2 cm)

MATERIALS

14 gold-filled jump rings, 16 gauge, 9/32-inch ID (A)

12 seamless gold-filled beads, 4 mm (B)

2 round stardust beads, 6 mm (C)

2 14kt gold-filled French hooks

INSTRUCTIONS

1 Open all 14 jump rings (A).

2 One at a time, place and close three open jump rings (A) through four seamless beads (B) each.

3 Place and close an open jump ring (A) through a stardust bead (C).

4 Place a jump ring (A) with four seamless beads (B) created in step 2 horizontally against the jump ring (A) with the stardust bead (C) created in step 3, as shown in figure 13.

FIGURE 13

5 Place and close an open jump ring (A) through the jump ring (A) with the stardust bead (C) created in step 3, pinning the horizontal jump ring (A) with four seamless beads (B) from step 4 in place, with two seamless beads (B) to either side of the chain, as shown in figure 14.

FIGURE 14

6 Place a jump ring (A) with four seamless beads (B) created in step 2 horizontally against the jump ring (A) added in step 5.

7 Place and close an open jump ring (A) through the jump ring (A) added in step 5, pinning the horizontal jump ring (A) with four seamless beads (B) from step 6 in place, with two seamless beads (B) to either side of the chain.

8 Place a jump ring (A) with four seamless beads (B), created in step 2, horizontally against the jump ring (A) added in step 7.

9 Place and close an open jump ring (A) through both the jump ring (a) added in step 7 and the loop of a French hook, pinning the horizontal jump ring (A) with four seamless beads (B) from step 8 in place, with two seamless beads (B) to either side of the chain.

10 Repeat steps 2 through 9 exactly to create a second matched earring.

Nautilus
Necklace

The one-of-a-kind focal bead in this necklace—created by a lampworking artist in Nova Scotia—makes it an absolute showstopper.

Finished Size Approximately 22 inches (55.9 cm) in circumference

MATERIALS

16-gauge sterling silver jump rings, as follows:

- 314 with an $^{11}/_{64}$-inch ID (A)
- 1 with a $^{9}/_{32}$-inch ID (B)

526 spring hard sterling silver jump rings, 21 gauge, $^{3}/_{32}$-inch ID (C)

21-gauge sterling silver jump rings, as follows:

- 20 with $^{1}/_{8}$-inch ID (D)
- 20 with $^{9}/_{64}$-inch ID (E)

10 sterling silver jump rings, 18 gauge, $^{5}/_{32}$-inch ID (F)

3 green lustre glass roller beads, 6 mm (G)

4 green iris glass roller beads, 6 mm (H)

3 seamless sterling silver beads, 4 mm (I)

Large focal bead with a small hole size, minimum 4.5 mm

Sterling silver infinity clasp, 13 x 7 mm

DESIGN TIP

Don't be afraid to go out and commission special focal beads of your own or track down focal bead substitutions; just make sure that your focal beads have at least a 4.5-mm hole. If not, you will have to use a bead reamer to clean/enlarge the hole to a point where you can fit a chain through.

INSTRUCTIONS

1 Open 160 of the jump rings (A), 322 of the jump rings (C), and all ten jump rings (F). Close the other 154 jump rings (A), the one jump ring (B), the 204 other jump rings (C), all 20 jump rings (D), and all 20 jump rings (E).

2 Place and close an open jump ring (F) through a roller bead (G).

3 Repeat step 2 a total of nine more times, placing and closing open jump rings (F) through each of the following: the remaining two glass roller beads (G), four glass roller beads (H), and three seamless silver beads (I).

4 Following the directions on page 24, create the 10 following Double Cable chains:

○ One consisting of a total of 27 pairs of jump rings (C)

○ One consisting of a total of 25 pairs of jump rings (C)

○ One consisting of a total of 23 pairs of jump rings (C)

○ One consisting of a total of 21 pairs of jump rings (C)

○ One consisting of a total of 19 pairs of jump rings (C)

○ One consisting of a total of 17 pairs of jump rings (C)

○ One consisting of a total of 15 pairs of jump rings (C)

○ One consisting of a total of 13 pairs of jump rings (C)

○ One consisting of a total of 11 pairs of jump rings (C)

○ One consisting of a total of nine pairs of jump rings (C)

5 One at a time, place and close two open jump rings (C) through the final pair of jump rings (C) from each of the 10 Double Cable chains created in step 4 and through two closed jump rings (D).

6 One at a time, place and close two open jump rings (C) through each of the pairs of closed jump rings (D) added to the end of each Double Cable chain in step 5 and through two closed jump rings (E).

7   One at a time, place and close two open jump rings (C) through each of the pairs of closed jump rings (E) added to the end of each Double Cable chain in step 6 and through one of the jump rings (F) with a bead, completed in step 3.

DESIGN TIP
From the longest to shortest Double Cable chain, the order of added beads is: (H) (G) (I) (G) (H) (I) (G) (H) (I) (H); however, you may use your own discretion for adding these beads.

8   One at a time, place and close two open jump rings (C) through each of the pairs of closed jump rings (C) from the end of each Double Cable chain and through the closed jump ring (B) to create a tassel of Double Cable chain. Note that you can attach the Double Cable chains to the closed jump ring (B) in order, from longest to shortest, if you wish, but this isn't necessary.

9   Following the directions on page 24, create a Double Cable chain that consists of approximately 13 pairs of jump rings (C). Note that it may be helpful to make this chain longer than it needs to be in order to feed it completely through the focal bead and then remove a small length of the Double Cable chain after it has been fed through the focal bead.

10 Place and close an open jump ring (A) through the pair of jump rings (C) from one end of the Double Cable chain created in step 9.

11 Feed the other end of the Double Cable chain completed in step 9 through one side of the focal bead, then through the closed jump ring (B) at the top of the chain tassel, then out through the other side of the focal bead, as shown in figure 1.

FIGURE 1

DESIGN TIP
You may find it helpful to tie the end of the Double Cable chain to a piece of string in order to feed it through the focal bead.

12 Place and close an open jump ring (A) through the pair of jump rings at the end of the Double Cable chain that has been fed through the focal bead, locking it in place.

Note that this chain should be as tight as possible, so it's perfectly all right to remove any extra jump ring (C) pairs from the end of the Double Cable chain. Again, attaching a string to the Double Cable chain can be very helpful for holding it in place during this kind of adjustment.

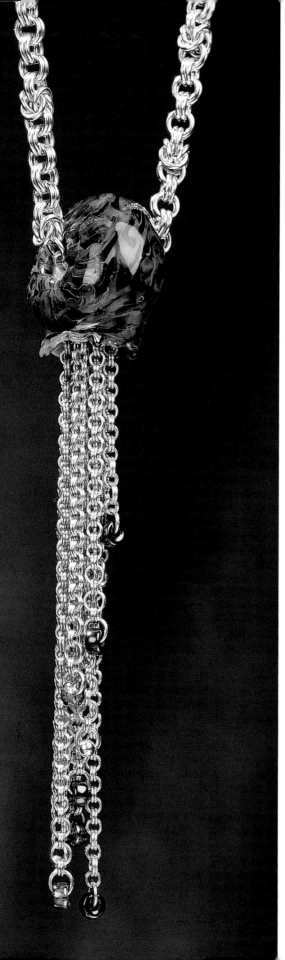

13　One at a time, place and close two open jump rings (A) through both the jump ring (A) from step 10 and two closed jump rings (A).

14　Fold the two closed jump rings (A) added in step 13 back, as in step 4 of the Byzantine pattern on page 30.

15　One at a time, place and close two open jump rings (A) through both the two closed jump rings (A) added in step 13 and two new closed jump rings (A), as shown in figure 2.

FIGURE 2

16　One at a time, place and close two open jump rings (A) through both the two closed jump rings (A) added in step 15 and two new closed jump rings (A).

17　Repeat step 16 a total of two more times, continuing the chain in the Double Cable style.

18　Fold the final two closed jump rings (A) back, as in step 4 of the Byzantine pattern.

19　Repeat steps 15 through 18 a total of eight more times, continuing the Half-Byzantine and Double Cable pattern.

20 One at a time, place and close two open jump rings (A) through both the final two closed jump rings (A) of the Half-Byzantine and Double Cable chain, which you folded back as the final repetition of step 18 during step 19, and two closed jump rings (A).

21 One at a time, place and close two open jump rings (A) through the two closed jump rings (A) added in step 20.

22 One at a time, place and close two open jump rings (A) through both the two jump rings (A) added in step 21 and the loop of a clasp.

23 Repeat steps 13 through 21, starting with the jump ring (A) added in step 12.

24 One at time, place and close two open jump rings (A) through both the two closed jump rings (A) added during the final repetition of step 21 and two closed jump rings (A).

ALTERNATE STEPS 10 AND 11

If you do not have a hollow focal bead, simply attach the Double Cable chain directly to the jump ring (B) of the tassel and then feed it through a regular focal bead, as shown in figure 3. Step 12 then creates a single attachment point for both sides of the Half-Byzantine and Double Cable chain.

FIGURE 3

141

Acknowledgments

I would like to acknowledge the contributions of the following people—I couldn't have done it without them! Ashley for her amazing patience and perception; my Dad for his unfaltering encouragement; Marian for his wealth of 3-D design knowledge; Spider at Spiderchain Jewelry for her generosity; Joe and Shelley at Metal Designz for their continued support; Jez for getting it all started; Polly, Alissa, and everyone else at Rings & Things; Judy at Natural Touch Beads; Kathi from Wichelt Imports/Mill Hill Beads; and last, but certainly not least, all my friends at Lark Books, including Terry Taylor, who is probably the most patient person on the planet! Lark editors Larry Shea and Mark Bloom caught what I missed, and for that I am grateful. My most sincere thanks also goes out to anyone whom I may have unintentionally forgotten, including all my fans around the world—especially the folks "down under!"

About the Author

Dylon Whyte has been studying and making original chain mail creations and patterns for 22 years. He has written and illustrated a self-published book on the construction of chain mail and is the co-author of the bestselling *Chain Mail Jewelry* (Lark, 2006). Dylon has created thousands of chain mail pieces: from full suits of armor containing one hundred thousand links to simple yet elegant earrings made from a single ring and several beads. Visit www.artofchainmail.com for more information about Dylon's creations.

Sources for Materials

Cousin Corporation—www.cousin.com

Fire Mountain Gems—www.firemountaingems.com

Forty Mile Gold—www.fortymilegold.ca

Glass Harp Gallery—www.glassharpgallery.com

Home Depot—www.homedepot.com

John Bead Corporation—www.johnbead.com

Lillian's Indian Crafts—www.lillianscrafts.com

Metal Designz—www.Metaldesignz.com

Mill Hill Beads—www.millhillbeads.com

Natural Touch Beads—www.naturaltouchbeads.com

Rings & Things—www.rings-things.com

Spiderchain Jewelry—www.spiderchain.com

Westrim Crafts—www.westrimcrafts.com

It's all on www.larkbooks.com

Can't find the materials you need to create a project? Search our database for craft suppliers & sources for hard-to-find materials.

Got an idea for a book? Read our book proposal guidelines and contact us.

Want to show off your work? Browse current calls for entries.

Want to know what new and exciting books we're working on? Sign up for our free e-newsletter.

Feeling crafty? Find free, downloadable project directions on the site.

Interested in learning more about the authors, designers & editors who create Lark books?

Manufacturers' Gauges

SPIDERCHAIN JEWELRY

(www.spiderchain.com)

American Wire Gauge—AWG-Brown & Sharpe

For all materials (sterling silver, gold fill, and jewelry brass):

Gauge	Inches	Millimeters
21	.028"	.72 mm
20	.032"	.81 mm
19	.036"	.91 mm
18	.040"	1.02 mm
17	.045"	1.15 mm
16	.051"	1.29 mm
15	.057"	1.45 mm
14	.064"	1.63 mm

METAL DESIGNZ

(www.metaldesignz.com)

Custom Wire Gauge—Closest match is British Imperial Standard-SWG

Sterling Silver

Gauge	Inches	Millimeters
20	0.031"	0.80 mm
18	0.045"	1.15 mm
16	0.063"	1.6 mm

Stainless Steel

Gauge	Inches	Millimeters
20	0.031"	0.80 mm
18	0.044"	1.13 mm
16	0.061"	1.56 mm

Bronze

Gauge	Inches	Millimeters
20	0.031"	0.80 mm
18	0.044"	1.13 mm
16	0.061"	1.56 mm

Copper

Gauge	Inches	Millemeter
20	0.031"	0.80 mm
18	0.047"	1.20 mm
16	0.061"	1.55 mm

Bright Aluminum

Gauge	Inches	Millimeters
18	0.046875"	1.191 mm
16	0.0625"	1.588 mm

Note: The gauges listed here are current as of the writing of this book, but are subject to change.

INDEX

Jump Ring Suppliers by Project

SPIDERCHAIN JEWELRY

Early Frost Necklace

Circle Drop Chandeliers

Beaded Persian Star Necklace

Connection Quartet

Mermaid's Tail

Drops of Jupiter

Centipede Bracelet & Earrings

Peacock Earrings

Arrowhead Wrap

Golden Lady Earrings

Zigzag Bracelet

Cable Cross Bracelet & Earrings

Red Carpet Cable Set

Grape Leaf Earrings

Orbital Earring Collection

Nautilus Necklace

METAL DESIGNZ

Gypsy Cuff Earrings

Bejewelled Eyeglass Chain

Moroccan Double Spiral Bracelet

Shell Spiral Earrings

Dancing Bells Anklet

Chain Gang

Flower Mail Choker & Bracelet

Bronze Age Bolo Tie

Zipper Charms

Andromeda Necklace